Rick Davis

Strategic Sales
in the Building Industry

A Service of

NAHB

BuilderBooks.com™
National Association of Home Builders
1201 15th Street, NW
Washington, DC 20005-2800
(800) 223-2665
www.builderbooks.com

Strategic Sales in the Building Industry
Rick Davis

Theresa Minch	Executive Editor
Jenny Stewart	Assistant Editor
Sharon Hamm	Copyeditor
Mike Bechetti	Illustrator
E Design Communications	Cover Designer

BuilderBooks at the National Association of Home Builders

THERESA MINCH	Executive Editor
DORIS TENNYSON	Senior Acquisitions Editor
JESSICA POPPE	Assistant Editor
JENNY STEWART	Assistant Editor
BRENDA ANDERSON	Director of Fulfillment
GILL WALKER	Marketing Manager
JACQUELINE BARNES	Marketing Manager

GERALD HOWARD	NAHB Executive Vice President and CEO
MARK PURSELL	Executive Vice President Marketing & Sales
GREG FRENCH	Staff Vice President, Publications and Affinity Programs

ISBN 0-86718-592-9

Printed in the United States of America

Library of Congress Cataloging-in-Publication Data

Davis, Rick, 1959-
  Strategic sales in the building industry / Rick Davis.
     p. cm.
  ISBN 0-86718-592-9
  1. Construction industry--Customer services. 2. Building
trades--Customer services. 3. Selling. 4. Sales management. 5.
Strategic planning. I. Title.
  HD9715.A2D32 2003
  690'.068'8--dc22
                                    2003020552

Disclaimer
This publication is designed to provide accurate and authoritative information in regard to the subject matter covered. It is sold with the understanding that the publisher is not engaged in rendering legal, accounting, or other professional service. If legal advice or other expert assistance is required, the services of a competent professional person should be sought.
> —From a Declaration of Principles jointly adopted by a Committee of the American Bar Association and a Committee of Publishers and Associations.

For further information, please contact:
BuilderBooks™
National Association of Home Builders
1201 15th Street, NW
Washington, DC 20005-2800
(800) 223-2665
Check us out online at: www.builderbooks.com

12/03 E Design Communications/Circle/Printer 2000

This book is dedicated to the memory of two sales leaders, my father, Mike Davis, and my father-in-law, Pete Naulty, two of the most fearless men I have ever known.

ABOUT THE AUTHOR

Rick Davis is the president of the Leaders Group, Inc., a training organization devoted solely to the pursuit of excellence for salespeople in the construction industry. Rick has been a professional salesperson in the building industry for two decades. After graduating from the University of Michigan with a major in Economics, he has continued to combine post-graduate studies and industry experience to uniquely mingle mainstream business concepts with psychology, philosophy, and ethics to create ideas that are universally accepted by salespeople. He has extensively studied the modern methods of training and motivational psychology. His programs work because the training participants welcome the ideas and style of delivery.

He has trained and coached thousands of salespeople, from Fortune 500 companies to Mom-and-Pop dealers. Because he has walked in the shoes of a building industry professional, his method of selling has been embraced by thousands of people. It is stuff that really works. In this book, he shares ideas focused on unique challenges to the construction industry.

For more information about additional training products or seminars, please contact The Leaders Group, Inc.; P.O. Box 408263; Chicago, IL 60640—or write for information at: info@leaders-group.net. Visit the website at www.leaders-group.net.

ACKNOWLEDGMENTS

I would like to thank my wife for her incredible support. She was my counselor, editor, friend, and psychologist during the project. Thank you, Meg. I love you. Thank you to my family for their wonderful love and support.

Special thanks to Tom Latourette, Mac Hines, and Bob Eckert, three unselfish individuals that I hope I can one day reciprocate for all of their support in my career.

I thank the folks at BuilderBooks, Theresa Minch and Jenny Stewart, for their support and outstanding efforts to publish this book. They do extraordinary work with limited resources.

I am indebted to Greg Bannon, Dave Barber, Lisa Clift, Tony DeJohn, Carlos Fernandez, Mark Hansen, Royce Kuntz, Cyndi Maxey, Brent Morris, Mike Reed, Larry Rich, Matt Riley, Steve Roth, Mark Schield, Matt Thompson, and Kathy Ziprik. Thank you all for your support during my journey.

I owe a special thanks to the good people at Specialty Building Resources, manufacturer of Style Solutions Millwork and Hy-lite Acrylic Block Windows.

I wish Aaron Slominski and Art Zapico were still here to see this book. I owe it to their families to recognize the mentoring and love that these two wonderful gentlemen provided a young man early in his career.

BuilderBooks would also like to thank Gian Hasbrock for reviewing this book.

TABLE OF CONTENTS

FIGURE LIST

INTRODUCTION

Perhaps the best way to begin a journey of confidence and courage in your sales career is with the recognition that, in this industry, we all do the same thing. Whether we are builders, remodelers, general contractors, trade contractors, dealers, distributors, lumberyards, manufacturers, or salespersons, we share the same task. Our job is to provide high-quality products and services to human beings so they can live in quality homes. We work in an industry in which virtually every salesperson promotes products and services to men and women who are members of the National Association of Home Builders (NAHB), an organization dedicated to helping builders and remodelers throughout the United States and the world.

Salespeople must recognize the importance of what builders and remodelers do. If we can't support the mission of these dedicated individuals who create American homes, then they have little chance to achieve credibility with their customers. As salespeople, we need to carefully consider the mission of our industry and how everyone involved can support that mission.

Rather than perceiving the industry as one in which we are competing ruthlessly for a piece of the pie, our first step toward happiness within the business is to recognize that our job is merely to help builders, remodelers, and designers create homes that satisfy consumers. This is probably not a gigantic step for most of us to take, at least in terms of a psychological or spiritual approach to selling. Despite the simplicity of this concept and the seemingly obvious truth inherent in the principle, however, most salespeople still struggle to behave in a way that eliminates the fear and pressure of quotas, deadlines, and responsibility.

Answering the Sales Challenge

The three forms of industry suffering introduced in Chapter 1 of this book are only a few of the many forms of "noise" that distract salespeople and cause negative emotions. Some salespeople invest their entire careers resisting change and the realities of our industry. The salespeople who discover how to accept these realities are happier and more successful in their careers.

The building industry is like the hockey game of business. Hockey is a fast-paced sport in which hitting the opponent is required for success and fighting is legal. Unlike most sports, in hockey there are no "time outs" during which a team can calmly reorganize and plan the next strategy. In hockey, noses get bloodied and the action never stops. Players think and react on the move. The success of a hockey player results from more than physical ability. The success of a hockey player results from mental conditioning that permits him or her to know what decision to make on split-second notice.

The building industry, like hockey, is fast paced and confrontational. Threats are a common tactic used in negotiations between customers and suppliers. The action takes place on a rough field of play. Some salespeople struggle their entire careers to achieve success, often changing jobs numerous times in hopes of finding the right opportunity. A minority of salespeople achieve reasonable success and comfort in their careers. And in the end, only a few emerge as the real superstars. When asked to what he attributed his success in hockey, the greatest player ever, Wayne Gretsky, said, "I don't go where the puck is. I go where the puck is going to be."

Gretsky's profound quote has implications for all of us in the rough hockey game of business that we call the construction industry. Only a few rare salespeople skate through the construction industry with the confidence and calm to know where the next opportunity will be. Many salespeople will assure you that they are confident in their skills, but they secretly have concerns and fears about their career. The construction industry is a tough business. Instead of praying for it to be easy, pray to find the strength to accept the challenges. You can't change the industry; you can only change *you*. And you can generate the strength to seek happiness and enjoyment in this business that creates homes for billions of people throughout the world.

Chapter 1 opens with some profound questions regarding the nature of the sales profession. Some of these questions are as profound to the profession as the questions of existence are to the meaning of life. These are questions about our profession that you should be asking yourself every day. I cannot promise to answer every one of the questions in black and white. Life is intuitive and humans are sensitive. This book is intended to heighten your awareness of the immense challenges of our profession and the building industry, and then to offer some solutions to those challenges.

The book is divided into three sections. The first section will heighten your awareness and prepare you for the sales challenges you will encounter in the building industry. The strategies and tactics outlined in the second section will provide specific actions that you can take to cope with the challenges. The final section offers methods to measure and track your progress. The ultimate objective of the book is to help you achieve the confidence and security that often eludes salespeople. This is a book of sales ideas to get you moving in the right direction. The rest is up to you.

CHAPTER ONE

SUFFERING
IN AN EVOLVING INDUSTRY

A wonderful icebreaker in a sales meeting is to ask people how they ended up in the construction industry. The answers to this question are as diverse as the people in the industry. What is *your* story? How did you end up in the construction industry? When you were growing up, you probably didn't plan to become a salesperson in this business. That so many of us end up in this wonderful industry, which, curiously, we enjoy and dislike at the same time, is an interesting phenomenon.

What makes some salespeople better than others? Have you recently experienced anger, fear, or frustration about your career? Why does it sometimes seem as though you are continually fighting just to keep your existing customers happy? How in the world can you find time to get new customers when you are so busy handling the difficult challenges that already exist? If you want to improve your performance, what are the steps you can take?

Nearly all salespeople admit that they suffer from habitual frustration as a result of challenges in the workplace. Discussions have revealed that negative emotions are not exceptions, but rather daily occurrences for many of us. To help deal with the persistent feeling of discomfort that plagues many salespeople, we must first determine why that feeling exists.

In the two decades I have been in the industry, I have concluded two things:

1. Most of us thoroughly enjoy being a part of the construction industry.
2. Most of us find this industry challenging and racked with intensity and emotion.

The challenges of the construction industry create suffering in the minds of its salespeople. That much is evident and proven by the responses of salespeople I have interviewed over many years. The causes of the suffering are, fortunately, curable. In fact, most of the frustration results from salespeople's unrealistic expectations. In other words, the emotional response to situations, rather than the situations themselves, causes the suffering. The construction industry (or any business or personal situation) does not inherently cause suffering.

The reality is that we do not always get what we want. Pain, suffering, and change are part of life. We can learn to acknowledge and accept these challenges, deal with them, and thus find happiness in life and our careers. All human beings can learn to deal with three types of suffering common in our business:

- The suffering of want.
- The suffering of negative events.
- The suffering created by resistance to change.

As you read this, you may not be comfortable with the term *suffering*. Unfortunately, there is probably not a good, comfortable word for anyone when it comes to admitting weakness or vulnerability. Yet fear and anger are real human feelings. When something causes fear and anger, the result is negative emotion. We could call this negative emotion any number of names—angst, frustration, and bad stuff. What we call the negative emotions really doesn't matter, as long as we recognize they exist, and we agree that it is better to avoid such emotions and seek happiness. Thus, we will call the negative emotions *suffering*. Be clear that suffering is not the event—it is not the cause. Suffering is the result. Suffering is our chosen reaction based upon our perception of the world. That is, we create our own suffering.

The nature of sales creates the *suffering of want* because the profession, by definition, requires the constant pursuit of more. The success of any organization is based upon growth and the need for more sales. Thus, the natural response for salespeople is to persistently experience a state of want in which, to succeed, we continually need more sales. The problem is that many salespeople never discover how to manage this perpetual want. The actual *need* for more, and the psychological *pressure* for more are separate entities to be

The nature of sales creates

the suffering of want

because the profession, by

definition, requires the

constant pursuit of more.

managed. Salespeople undoubtedly need to sell something, which creates actual pressure. Psychological suffering results when we feel helpless in our ability to achieve constant sales growth. One objective of this book is to help those in sales manage the seemingly insatiable need for more.

Actual negative events—e.g., late deliveries, traffic jams, or an angry customer threatening to stop doing business with us—create the second cause of suffering. One might expect that the only available emotions to a negative event are fear or anger. But we as human beings are much more resilient than we credit ourselves. When we consider some of the events with which individuals have dealt in their lives—loss of a loved one, a devastating health problem, the bombing of the twin towers—it hardly seems we should have difficulty handling minor challenges such as a late delivery or a temporarily angry customer. When we stop to consider the real causes of our responses of fear and anger to negative events, we realize that we always have choices about how we deal with those events. We can allow them to control our emotions, or we can control our reaction and make the best of a bad situation.

Resistance to change creates the third cause of suffering for salespeople. I have worked with hundreds of salespeople who openly discuss their fear of changes, such as potential realignment of their territories, sudden economic shifts, or the constant changes of computer technology, to name only a few. The problem is that salespeople often resist the inevitability of constant change, hoping there will be an end to the cycle. But the winds of change are constant and unavoidable. We need to learn to expect change and plan to adapt rather than fight the forces of the universe.

When we experience negative emotions, we must question whether we or external events are the cause of our feelings. In fact, nobody can make us feel badly without our permission. Our suffering results from the fears we create in response to external events.

In the construction industry, literally hundreds of daily events might be cause for us to create suffering. To describe all these events would be useless. Four situations that most commonly cause suffering for salespeople are:

1. Complex distribution channels
2. Price sensitivity
3. The impact of industry consolidation
4. Technological evolution

Learning the strategies in this book will help overcome these and hopefully other forms of suffering.

Complex Distribution Channels

Perceptions of distribution channels can create two forms of suffering—negative events and resistance to change. In some cases, salespeople work in markets in which manufacturers have made decisions regarding distribution methods that cause intense competition for salespeople (negative event).

As salespeople, we want to believe that life is simple. We would prefer calm and order, which makes our jobs easier. We wish we could at least count on structured distribution channels to mirror our expectations of simplicity (resistance to reality). Our discussions of distribution channels frequently suggest that a standardized method actually exists. Our perception is that the channels of distribution are—or at least *should be*—linear and simplistic, neat and tidy, as shown in Figure 1.1.

Perhaps there was such a time when the distribution of materials was simple and easy to comprehend. But if such a time ever existed, it is long past. Today, our industry is complicated by thousands of factors, ranging from industry regulation to incompetent behaviors, from technological advancement to highway traffic. The complications are endless. Yet we strive to make order out of business by creating a structure in our minds that is not mirrored by reality. In the real world, distribution channels for construction materials are convoluted, as shown in Figure 1.2.

The methods of distribution can be as simple as a manufacturer selling directly to a builder. The methods of distribution can be as complex as a manufacturer selling to a two-step distributor, who resells to a dealer, who resells to an installer, who resells to the builder—not to mention the inclusion

FIGURE 1.1 The Dream World

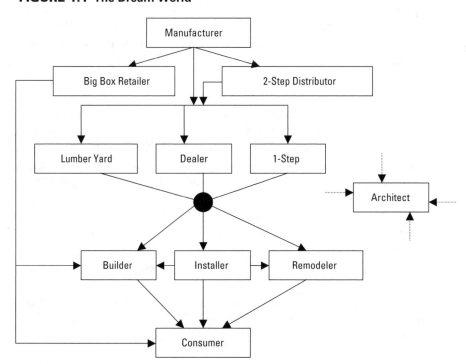

FIGURE 1.2 The Real World

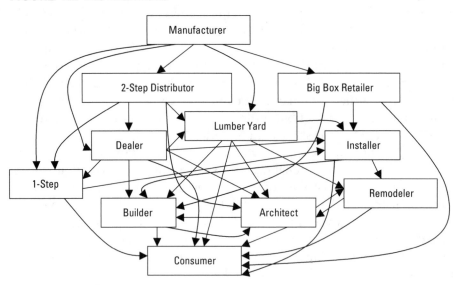

in the chain of an architect who made a product recommendation that directed the product-selection process.

The causes for diversity and confusion of distribution channels are as complex as the channels themselves. Each salesperson's market probably presents unique challenges, thus creating specific methods of distribution. For example, if you live in a major metropolitan market, you might have situations in which manufacturers avoid the costs of a two-step-distribution middleman and sell directly to dealers. The volume of demand justifies that model; whereas in a rural market, because of sporadic product demand, the very same manufacturer may choose to distribute products to two-step distributors who resell products to dealers.

Installation methods often create pressures on distribution channels. For example, a manufacturer of glass-curtain wall systems will achieve success only by selling directly to a dealer who is capable of installing products on a jobsite. The evolving trend in the industry indicates that more and more material suppliers will furnish installation services to support the growth of product sales.

Product differentiation is also a factor in the methods of distribution for a manufacturer. For example, fireplaces are products that manufacturers frequently sell to two-step distributors because of the need for regional warehousing of materials. An individual dealer cannot justify the inventory cost for a large warehouse of fireplaces.

Some products are sold directly to dealers who sell directly to builders. This way eliminates the added burden of costs that the two-step model would create for the builder. Some of the products that lend themselves to successful "one-step" distribution are windows, doors, lumber, and millwork.

Some products *appear* to be sold in a one-step model, although a middleman actually exists in the form of an installer. Products that are commonly sold by installers to builders include wood flooring, vinyl siding, and roofing. If an installer is the purchaser of products, then, in reality, a middleman exists between the builder and the dealer.

In many cases, the methods by which even a single manufacturer distributes materials become quite complex (Figure 1.3). Some manufacturers employ direct sales to builders and big-box national chains. Some manufacturers employ two-step distributors and dealers, and lumberyards and commercial sales divisions, all at the same time.

> The diversity of definitions of dealer types and distribution methods could fill an entire book. The glossary in this book provides a foundation for the terminology used here, which may not be the exact terminology to which you have become accustomed. For example, in some markets, local custom is to call a lumberyard a retailer, an organization that sells lumber "directly" to builders. In numerous other markets, the term retailer signifies an organization that sells to consumers.

If you are confused, then consider yourself well-educated on the "standard" methods of distribution that exist in the building industry. In fact, there are no simple methods. Suffering occurs when we deny the existence of the nonlinear and refuse to accept the spaghetti-like distribution model that mirrors reality. Our success as salespeople hinges on our ability to

FIGURE 1.3 The "Sales" World

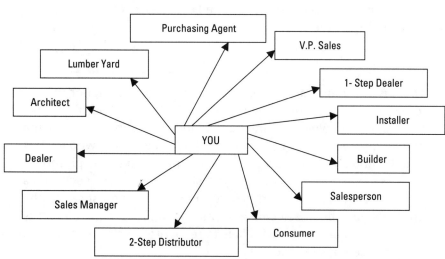

accept reality and sell to every entity within the distribution model. Sales-people who concentrate too closely on only one segment of the distribution channel eventually discover that their skills are inade-quately developed for career-growth opportunities.

Our success as salespeople hinges on our ability to accept reality and sell to every entity within the distribution model.

This is a central theme of strategic selling: We do not always get to choose the environment in which we will compete. Our opportunities for success will be improved as we develop skills that prepare us for dif-ferent types of customers and different situations. Thus, we must be prepared to adapt our selling style and strategies to the different types of customers we will encounter.

Like a hockey game, the real world is complex and challenging. To the casual observer, a hockey game is marked by disorder and chaos, with skaters randomly chasing a tiny, moving black disk while they're knocking into each other. Periodically, a random success occurs, but, for the most part, the game is chaotic. A casual fan (like me) is unable to understand the complexities and subtleties of a hockey game. A casual observer to the building industry would be equally inept at understanding the complexities and subtleties of the environment. The challenge for us as salespeople is to recognize that we are not casual observers of the game of construction industry sales. We are players in the game, and we need to take more than a casual interest in observing reality.

If distribution channels were accurately depicted by Figure 1.1, then you would expect that builders' decisions are influenced only by salespeople working for dealers, 1-steppers, and lumberyards. In reality, builders are influenced by manufacturers, dealers, architects, other salespeople, and other factors within the distribution channel. The following case studies demonstrate that this simplistic model fails to mirror reality. They provide excellent examples of sales experiences and the diverse ways in which power is wielded in the market.

The custom-home architect. Eric, architect and designer of cus-tom homes in Chicago, selects key products on behalf of his cus-tomers. His involvement in projects includes supervision of the builder involved in the construction. Any salesperson who wishes to sell windows, millwork, cabinets, lighting fixtures, plumbing fixtures, and other designer items should expect to seek Eric's approval before submitting bids to the builder. In most cases, the products have been selected and priced long before the builder is involved. A salesperson who fails to recognize Eric's influence has little chance for sales success.

The lumber landlord. A prominent midwestern lumberyard possessed extensive landholdings that were sold to builders and developers in the suburban area of a major metropolitan market. Builders who purchased the land were free to purchase their materials from any lumberyard in the area. The fact is that most builders purchased goods from this same lumberyard that sold them the land. The lumberyard packaged the sale of the property and materials in such a way that the builders were faced with an "offer they could not refuse." A salesperson who wanted to achieve success in that market needed to know that the lumberyard was the key.

The sales superstar. In rare instances, salespeople single-handedly sell between 5 and 10 times more product than the average salesperson. Although the average dimensional lumber salesperson is happy to sell $2 million or $3 million per year, a few rare salespeople in metropolitan markets throughout the United States sell more than $1 million of lumber and related materials . . . per month! The average window salesperson sells less than $1 million per year, yet a Chicago salesperson for a prominent window brand *lost* a single account in 2001 that accounted for more than $1 million in sales. Despite the loss, the salesperson, John, increased his sales in 2002 by *more than* $1 million. He was the top performer for the window manufacturer and finished the year with close to $7 million in window sales! John asserted that the secret to his success is that he "never stops prospecting and knows as many people in the market as he can."

The product installer. An Atlanta dealer of formed polyurethane millwork materials virtually controlled the distribution of exterior millwork materials to the most prominent builders in the market. The builders appreciated the convenience of managing their labor costs by allowing the installer to take all the risk of variable total costs. If a formed millwork manufacturer wanted to enter the Atlanta market, the manufacturer had better realize that the installer held the key. The only alternative for a manufacturer or dealer would be direct sales to the large-volume builders who included the installation of materials.

The big builder program. Many manufacturers are developing programs aimed at selling materials to the largest volume builders in the country. The objective for many of these programs is not to sell the materials directly to builders, but rather to create national agreements that bind the builders and manufacturers while permitting the inclusion of an intermediary dealer to handle the logistics of inventory, delivery, and (potentially) installation. After the agreements have been reached, the manufacturers and builders select a local dealer by mutual agreement.

> One sales leader, Scott, working for a manufacturer of polyurethane millwork, was able to strike a national contract with one of the largest builders in the country. The contract conflicted with the arrangement made by the Atlanta installer in the previous example. The installer was forced to choose, either to lose a significant builder account, or to switch all of his purchases to Scott's company. He chose the latter, and thus the byproduct of Scott's effort was that his employer was able to convert a large block of business to his company in Atlanta.

The common ingredient in all of the case studies listed is that a unique sales relationship dictated the power of the situation. Your ability to succeed is not as influenced as you may believe by your position on the distribution channel, but is determined by the sales abilities that you choose to develop and employ. The complexities of distribution channels need not create complexities in your mind. You can easily overcome the complexities by remembering one simplicity upon which all sales success relies: *A single salesperson has the power regardless of their position in the distribution channel to dramatically influence any audience with whom he comes into contact.* A study conducted by ProSales Magazine identified 16 different factors that influence product decisions, 10 of which wield strong influence. A single salesperson has the ability to identify the single most important factors for each customer, thus allowing the salesperson to become influential in the decision-making process.

In the last two case studies, it is evident that situations arise in which power shifts can occur as a result of superior salesmanship. In every case study, power was "localized." It has been said, "all politics are local." The profession of selling is no different. In each case study, a talented sales leader was at the core of the success. As a salesperson, you are in a position to discover the same type of power that will help you rise to heights of success in your market that you never before imagined.

Price Sensitivity in the "Toughest" Market

The strategies listed in this book will help you deal with the most prevalent source of suffering that occurs in the construction industry, if not the entire profession of selling—price. No other single subject creates as much suffering as price. Price is the benchmark by which most salespeople determine the nature of their marketplace. I have had the pleasure of discovering this characteristic while conducting seminars in dozens of cities throughout the country. During those seminars, I have learned from salespeople who represent hundreds of cities in the United States.

You may be pleased to know that, during my travels, I have learned from salespeople exactly where the "toughest" market for selling is located. I first discovered that the toughest market in the United States is Decatur, Illinois. I learned this early in my career when, as you might expect, I was in Decatur, Illinois. The salesperson with whom I was working at the time told me, "Decatur is the toughest market." I had no reason to argue with him at the time, but I later found out that he was not necessarily correct.

During subsequent travels, I discovered that other markets were the "toughest" in the country. I was informed that Rockford, Illinois is the toughest market. I was later told that Columbus, Ohio is the toughest market. I have been fortunate to discover that the toughest market is also Los Angeles, Chicago, Charleston, Detroit, and nearly 100 other cities. If you're wondering how I might have come across these valuable pieces of enlightened information, here is the answer: I have learned that the toughest market is where I happen to be on any given day! The salespeople in every market consistently tell me that they are in the toughest market.

Naturally, whatever the claims, every city can't be the toughest market. So I decided to do some qualitative research. There had to be some way to determine why so many salespeople believe they are in the toughest market, and by which criteria they gauge their assertions. You will be interested to know that the number one reason people stated for rating their market the toughest was price. Salespeople have frequently commented, "every builder is only concerned with price." I am often told, "price is king." Hundreds of salespeople have told me that builders do not even want to meet them until they are satisfied that their prices are competitive. In fact, salespeople commonly say that price has become more important than ever to builders. Even without quantitative data, salespeople subjectively assert that price is the most important criteria by which builders choose products and by which the difficulty of their market is determined. But we all know that other factors are equally, if not more, important than price to builders—product quality, supplier service, and product availability. Yet salespeople prefer to reject the evidence provided by objective data and quantitative measurement.

Price suffering comes in all forms. Salespeople react fearfully and submissively to customers at the first mention of price during negotiations, for fear of losing a "much needed" sale (suffering of want). Salespeople also struggle with periodic price increases and last-minute requests for price concessions (suffering of resistance to change). The most common agony for salespeople results from the sales that are lost because they could not match a competitor's price (suffering of negative events). Highly skilled salespeople have discovered, however, that the price, while important, is not the cause of lost sales as frequently as one might expect. The truth is that price becomes a critical issue for those salespeople who lack a strategic game plan.

Industry Consolidation

A large part of human suffering results from a resistance to change. Yet the only constant on which we can depend is change. One change that is occurring in the construction industry is a rapid movement toward consolidation. Large builders are becoming larger. Large networks of dealers are becoming larger. Leading manufacturers are increasing market share.

The construction industry may still be unique in that even now it provides opportunities for the quaint mom and pop businesses. Many builders work from their homes and represent very small organizations. The great majority of product dealers throughout the country are privately held organizations that cater to the needs of their local market. So although it is pleasing to recognize that the distribution of building materials temporarily remains a cottage industry, it is naïve to ignore current market trends.

Salespeople should prepare themselves for the certainty of market consolidation. One big-box retailer boasts that it sells 40 percent of all lighting fixtures in the United States. According to *ProSales* magazine, only one dealer (chain) in the country sold more than $1 billion in fixtures in 1998. The May 2003 issue of *ProSales* lists 6 dealers who sold more than $1 billion, the largest one topping out at $2.4 billion. In 1995, the top 10 builders in the United States produced 6 percent of all homes. In 2002, only seven years later, the top 10 builders doubled their market share, producing 12 percent of the 1.65 million homes in the United States. Nearly every industry expert believes this consolidation trend will continue.

Consolidation is occurring by virtue of acquisition, not necessarily sales growth. In other words, big fish are being bought up by bigger fish. The result is that many companies are wisely striving to capitalize on consolidation by establishing relationships based upon regional and national alliances. Large organizations are persistently seeking opportunities to purchase smaller organizations. Manufacturers are structuring national purchasing contracts with large-volume builders and dealers.

The impact of consolidation on your sales career may be significant. You may discover that, when your current employer sells the company, overnight you are suddenly working for a new employer. A national purchasing agreement may supercede a strong relationship you have with a local builder when your customer is sold to a bigger builder. An exclusive marketing arrangement with a manufacturer may quickly vanish when a national dealer chain decides to enter your market. The challenge of big-box retailers offering services to builders and remodelers will grow. The impact of consolidation will continue to affect your career more, not less, in the coming years.

The only preparation for consolidation that salespeople can make at a local level is to ensure that they have exceptional sales skills and a solid knowledge of their market. Career security is no longer demonstrated in the form of sales volume. Career security is demonstrated by salespeople who have strong, long-term relationships with numerous builders, remodelers, and architects in their marketplace. Career security is demonstrated by the development and growth of personal selling skills that will always be valued in the market.

The Evolving Industry of Technology

Perhaps the most significant evolution in the construction industry over the past two decades has been the explosion of technological innovation. This evolution has dramatically affected salespeople's suffering created by resistance to change in two ways. The first is that industry technology has evolved so rapidly that the ways in which houses are constructed, and the resulting quality of those houses, has been redefined. The second is that computer technology has changed the way business is conducted.

Technology innovations include engineered lumber; vinyl products; hurricane-resistant, high-impact glass; synthetic house wraps; thermally efficient glass; high-performance paints; cement-board construction components; and many more. Product innovations have provided both a boon and bane to builders. The technological explosion has allowed builders to produce better homes more efficiently than their forefathers. Conversely, there has been a dramatic rise in regulation, along with confusion regarding the best use of the new technologies.

The bane for builders provides a boon to salespeople. The need for talented and knowledgeable salespeople is significantly increased by the emerging technology. Builders, architects, and other industry professionals have become more reliant than ever on the training and knowledge that skilled salespeople provide. Of course, the flipside to the issue is that salespeople not only need to understand the evolving technology of the products they sell, but they also need to communicate the information effectively. The strategies and tactics listed later in this book will aid you as you prepare for such presentations.

The emergence of computer technology has dramatically revolutionized the ways in which salespeople perform their jobs. In the old days, a mere 20 years ago, fax machines were new gimmicks, and personal computers were hardly on the business horizon. Today, a salesperson has to choose among extensive productivity tools ranging from personal computers to spreadsheets, from portable data devices to database software, from cell phones to fax machines in the home. The unique aspect of the computer technology boom is that hardly any productivity device has become obsolete; new tools and options merely continue to be added to the mix. Purchase orders are still placed by way of US mail, telephone, fax, the Internet, and more. Instead of relying on only one form of technology, skilled salespeople are forced to understand all forms of technology and utilize the methods that are most convenient to their customers.

The technological revolution has created a resistance to change that is palpable. The related suffering for salespeople comes in the form of resistance to mandates by employers to use computers, in the form of multiple phone numbers and voice mails, in the form of competitive challenges. If your competitor is better equipped than you to manage massive amounts of data, what does that bode for your career future?

Most salespeople still do not use spreadsheets or database software to track their client activity. Most salespeople only sparingly use their personal computers to enhance work productivity. Technology offers a great opportunity to improve personal productivity, but resistance to change often hampers salespeople's individual growth. The discussion of quantification and performance measurement later in the book will help you understand how you can use technology to enhance your personal productivity.

The Elimination of Suffering

The causes of suffering seem to be at the heart of the sales challenge. If you can relieve the suffering caused by want, negative events, and resistance to change, then you will enjoy a more satisfying career. You may believe that the suffering is insurmountable and unavoidable. Read on and you will discover that you are in control of your emotions. You have the ability to discover happiness in our very challenging industry.

CHAPTER TWO

CREATING
A VISION OF SUCCESS

Current training methods in the construction industry have done little to alleviate the suffering of salespeople. The primary method of sales training in the construction industry during the past 30 years has focused on "features and benefits." Manufacturers, distributors, and dealers sponsor regular training events during which product features and benefits are discussed *ad nauseam*. I have nothing against highlighting features that are important to builders and contractors. In fact, salespeople must have strong product knowledge to succeed. Unfortunately, the product knowledge and rote feature-benefit presentations do not necessarily concentrate on the issues that are really important to customers and prospects.

The presentations of most salespeople would be more accurately described as product "dumps," desperate attempts to convince customers that their products are superior to all others. In feature-benefit presentations, salespeople recite a list of features to prospects with little concern about how the message is being received. They talk verbosely about features that are important to consumers, yet of little importance to the industry professionals to whom they are presenting. For example, a salesperson might talk exhaustively about the energy efficiency of any number of construction materials, while a builder, being more interested in installation issues, quickly loses interest. Another salesperson might describe the wonderful self-cleaning feature of the electric oven, which is certainly an important feature to a homeowner. But, unless the builder can sell that same benefit to the consumer, it is not a feature that will gain the builder's interest.

If you asked most salespeople, they would deny that they are reciting irrelevant features to their customers. In spite of these assertions, however, listeners to these monotonous presentations would tell you that they come across as desperate sales attempts. The secret to selling new customers begins with the ability to ask questions. For instance, using the example of the oven, a salesperson would be wise to first discover what existing challenges the builder faces. If delivery is the most important issue, then the salesperson should focus on delivery issues in the presentation. If installation is a concern, then the salesperson will obviously discuss installation issues. If the builder states that customers do not appreciate the special touches included in the builder's homes, then a salesperson might focus on a training session in which he or she shares the special consumer features (e.g., self-cleaning oven) with the builder's salespeople.

Most salespeople never get far enough into the sales process to discover these wonderful opportunities, choosing instead to leap into the presentation and pricing processes too quickly. As a matter of principle, salespeople believe they must offer some form of a presentation, if for no other reason than to preserve their self-respect. Thus, they spout the obligatory features and benefits, and the builder accepts the presentation as a matter of courtesy while anxiously awaiting the real information, the price.

The feature-benefit sales style results in a strong reliance on price competitiveness. Salespeople who are overly mindful of product features place themselves at a disadvantage in which customers can easily shift the focus back to price issues. When builders demonstrate no enthusiasm for product features, salespeople often recognize no alternative methods to provide value and fearfully assume that the only resolution to the conflict is a reduction in price. Naturally, to assert that situations never arise in which a customer legitimately merits a lower price would be naïve. What concerns many sales managers, business owners, and suppliers, though, is that they receive requests for lower prices from salespeople almost exclusively with no supporting documentation or justification. Salespeople confidently assert, "The builder told me the price was too high," failing to recognize that the builder might merely be testing the waters. An eventual reduction in price tells builders that there was room to move in the first place, leaving them wondering whether they should be mistrustful of future pricing from the salesperson. They further wonder whether they ultimately received the best price, concerned that they may have left money on

An eventual reduction in price tells builders that there was room to move in the first place, leaving them wondering whether they should be mistrustful of future pricing from the salesperson.

the table. The result of this negotiation tactic is lost revenue for suppliers and, more importantly, insecurity for builders.

The price negotiation is a reaction to which salespeople have become accustomed. The problem with constant price negotiation is that everyone sacrifices profits in the end. In the real world, builders often have the ability to pass higher costs on to their customers, while the manufacturer and supplier many not be able to recoup lost revenues of even a single percentage point. In the real world, even a single percentage point reduction in price is the equivalent of up to 33 percent of a supplier's profit (see Figure 2.1).

You might quickly surmise that, were builders to read this section, they would instantly tell you that they do, in fact, expect you to negotiate and reduce your prices whenever possible. The truth is that many builders prefer that you wisely use your time and theirs. The most successful builders are not trying to monopolize your organization's time and resources. They recognize that if you use your resources inefficiently for one builder, each and every builder pays, either directly or indirectly, with higher prices, poor service, or both. The best builders in your market also will agree that your organization needs to make a reasonable profit.

A prevalent behavior of salespeople in the building industry has been a persistent willingness to aimlessly bid on projects. Hundreds of salespeople throughout the country are asking builders these words every day: "Do you have anything I can bid on?" Many of these salespeople will tell you that their intent is to make the builder a long-term customer, even though their behavior suggests they are submissively asking for permission to gain a short-term, project-based relationship. Project sales are like

FIGURE 2.1 Profit/Loss Statement for XYZ Distribution

Revenue (100%)	$1.00
Material	$ .78
People	.09
Overhead	.08
Cost of money/bad debt	.02
Total Cost of Operations (97%)	$ .97
Net Profit (3%)	$ .03

This simplistic profit/loss statement represents the typical profit model for hundreds of material supply dealers throughout the United States. For every dollar of revenue, a material supplier invests 97 cents for the cost of operations, leaving 3% profit. Some very profitable dealers operate on a slightly larger margin, while others do not fare as well. In this scenario, every 1% reduction in the price of the goods sold represents a loss of one-third of the dealer's profits (i.e., 1%/3% = 1/3).

one-night stands, whereas the building of a strong business relationship is like a courtship.

When you approach a builder in hopes of merely bidding on the next project, the builder is only too happy to provide sets of blueprints or a material list from which you can price. The result of this behavior is a poor use of time, not to mention a career based in fear. You discover that you close only a small percentage of your bids, although you invest significant time preparing them. This crap-shoot cycle always creates the perpetual suffering of want noted in the previous chapter. The psychological implication of this approach is a perception that the builder is always in control and the salesperson is always the victim. Difficult as it may be to believe, the feature-benefit-price cycle, while seemingly placing all the power in the hands of the customer, is a sales style motivated by selfish behavior and greed. In other words, the salesperson concentrates solely on ways to make a sale to alleviate his or her personal suffering.

> Project sales are like one-night stands, whereas the building of a strong business relationship is like a courtship.

The solution to the feature-benefit-price cycle of selling is simple. Salespeople need to create strategies to replace the traditional (reactive) fear-based approach of "bid and pray." We need to replace the feature-benefit-price cycle with a vision that is more inclusive of the needs of all entities involved in the business transaction. The strategies and tactics in this book are focused on ways we can become more assertive in our sales style, while we offer a heartfelt approach to the profession. The strategies support a vision in which our sole focus is to help everyone in the process become happier and more successful. The suffering of want (for oneself) is replaced with a sincere desire to alleviate the suffering of others. The result of this altruistic approach is an elimination of suffering and an elevation of career success.

Selling from the Heart

To discover happiness in our careers, we must consciously choose to replace suffering with alternative forms of emotion. Two emotions that can help alleviate suffering are *empathy* and the *desire for personal growth*. The problem with the feature-benefit-price cycle is that it persistently creates fear, simply because salespeople who use it limit customer feedback. If we are busy talking and avoiding our customers' feedback, then we will definitely lack an understanding of our customers' needs. The natural outcome from this lack of knowledge is fear.

To achieve happiness, we must first recognize that we are not alone when it comes to dealing with fear. Our customers, coworkers, and employers all encounter challenges, too. Successful salespeople have discovered that one key to happiness is to help others eliminate suffering in their careers. The most successful salespeople are those who can help others eliminate fear. And to help others, we must first eliminate our selfish behaviors.

Here is the litmus test by which you can determine whether you behave selfishly with your customers. Answer this question: *If you want to sell your customer more of your product, what do you first need to know about your customer?* Before you read on, jot down a few ideas to help clarify your answer. Take the time to think about the question, and determine how you would really answer it if were you taking an oral exam.

> Successful salespeople have discovered that one key to happiness is to help others eliminate suffering in their careers.

When you are fully satisfied with the answer, ask yourself a second question: *If you want to truly help your customer become more profitable, what do you need to know about your customer?* After you have answered that question to your own satisfaction, read on.

What You Need to Know

In countless seminars, I have asked the first of the two questions and consistently received the same answers. Salespeople instantly respond that the data they need to successfully sell to a customer include information related to product usage and supplier information. Salespeople state they need to know what products the prospect currently uses. They say they need to understand what the prospect currently likes and dislikes about competitors' products, and how satisfied the prospect is with current service and delivery issues.

I humbly assert that these issues are rather selfish. Such answers to the first question merely help *these salespeople* design *their* sales approaches.

When seminar participants answer the second question, after some confusion, they begin to seriously contemplate how to help their prospects increase profits. They realize they need to understand issues relative to prospects' overall profitability, such as their competitive challenges, marketing visions, business models, labor costs, target audiences, and more.

I then ask a third question, and many participants are surprised by their answers, "Shouldn't your answer to the second question have been the same as your answer to the first question?" After some silence, most agree. At this point, they are finally recognizing the benevolence that creates profitability for their customers and ultimately for themselves.

"If you really want to help your customers in a business-to-business sales environment, shouldn't your relationship focus on ways in which you can help your customers become more profitable?" This is the moment when many salespeople blurt out, "Sure! And that is the exact reason customers constantly negotiate for a better price—so they can be more profitable . . ." This viewpoint negates the many other ways in which you thought you could help your customers fulfill their visions.

Price is only one way to help your customers fulfill their visions.

Salespeople neglect to realize their essential role in ensuring that the business transaction is accomplished to the mutual benefit of *all* entities. As a common practice in seminars, when I talk about the importance of "matching needs," I quickly ask, "Whose needs do we need to match in the profession of selling?" The instantaneous answer is always "the customer's." After a brief pause, I will then ask, ". . . the customer's, and. . . ?"

Participants quickly note that the "supplier's needs" must be met, and eventually someone notes that the "salesperson's needs" should also be satisfied. Our responsibility is to ensure that three parties enjoy mutual benefit from the transaction—the customer, the supplier, and the salesperson. The problem is that most of us do not understand the vision either of our cus-

FIGURE 2.2 The Needs of the Three Entities in the Business Relationship

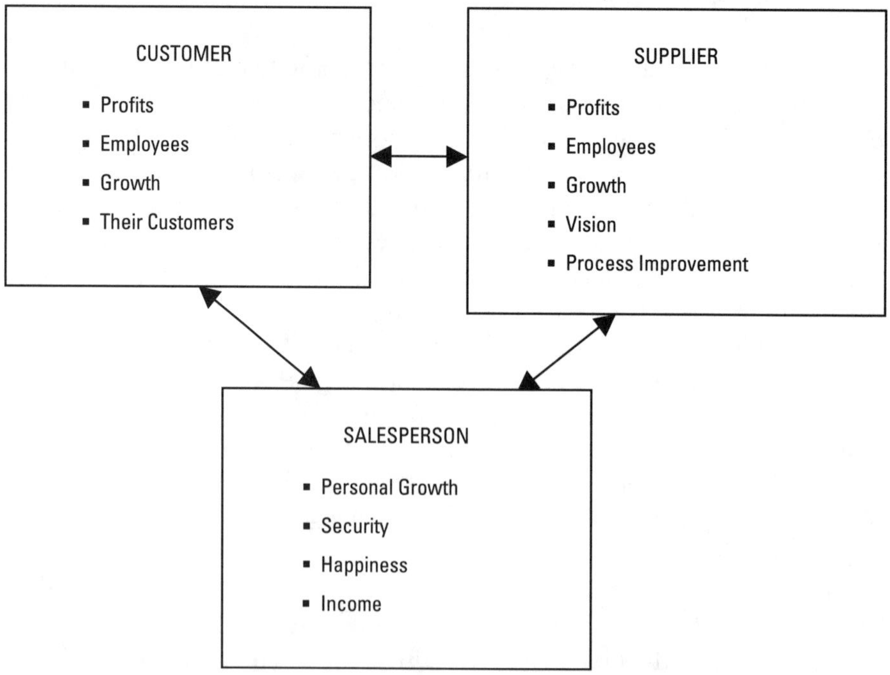

The responsibility of fulfilling the needs of all entities in the sales process can be very exciting. The customer's vision can include more than merely providing profits, but can also entail satisfying the employees and culture of the organization. The same is true for the supplier. A salesperson should recognize that they have the opportunity to positively affect the quality of life for hundreds of people by satisfying the needs of all entities in the business relationship.

tomers or their suppliers. The majority of this chapter focuses on understanding the visions of our customers, the suppliers, and ourselves as salespeople. The chapter will conclude with a discussion about ways to ensure that our behavior aligns with our own visions and those of our target audience.

The Customer's Vision—Profit

Although many salespeople believe that the value of their relationship with customers is best measured by the volume of the business, customers value the relationship much differently. They measure the profitability of the relationship. This perspective seems obvious, and yet salespeople continually focus their sales effort on issues related to product features, price, and sales volume. The most important issue *to your customers* is the bottom-line profit. If you want to become a resource to eliminate suffering for your customers, then sell the profitability of the relationship.

Your job as the salesperson is to promote a *profit model*. A profit model is a formal term for an informal sales process. Every transaction generates some form of profit (or loss) for the customer. For example, a popular brand of product that helps builders increase the sales of their homes might be worth more in long-term profits than a lesser-known product, despite the lower price of the lesser-known product.

A profit model is the value of the transactions and business relationship between the supplier and customer. Salespeople may sell any of five popular profit models to customers and prospects:

- Price
- Product quality
- Service
- Value added
- Partnership

The most commonly promoted profit model is *price,* although most salespeople would hardly call price a profit model. They would instead state that the customer seeks the best price and that their job is to offer the best price possible. Salespeople frequently behave in a manner that suggests their responsibility is to negotiate with the supplier on behalf of the customer. The problem is that, in that situation, only two of three entities win—the customer and the salesperson, while the supplier is left with the lowest possible margins and a potential deficit. More important to the discussion is that salespeople are frequently reacting unnecessarily to the price issue.

If customers sought only to purchase products as cheaply as possible, then obviously the industry would quickly reach a point at which only the cheapest suppliers of materials would be left standing. This is clearly not the situation, as evidenced by the fact that some of the most popular products sold today are virtually the most expensive in their respective categories. Thus, we can say with certainty that price, while definitely important, is not the most important consideration for our customers. Salespeople throughout the world nevertheless behave in a way that supports one single belief: that price is the only consideration.

Studies have demonstrated that builders select products based upon numerous criteria, including product quality, brand awareness, service, supplier relationships, product availability, and price.

In a study conducted by *ProSales* magazine, builders noted that on-time delivery was the most important criterion when selecting a suppler. A salesperson who is able to successfully manage delivery expectations instantly gains the upper hand on their competitor. The same study noted that price, the third most important criterion, was only slightly more important than knowledgeable salespeople and loyalty to past relationships. It would be interesting to conduct a study among salespeople. I suspect they would overwhelmingly rate price as the most important factor for their customers while underestimating the numerous other factors that influence decisions. There are many factors that influence decisions. Price is merely one among many.

Product quality is naturally an important factor in purchasing decisions. What constitutes product quality is less clear. In some cases, brand recognition is enough to establish product quality. For example, some builders prefer to install popular products in their homes even in lieu of better products that are offered at a lower price. *In other words, customers might perceive that a product has more quality even if it isn't better.* This paradox explains to salespeople that perceptions of quality are relative to each individual.

Many salespeople have found themselves in situations in which they have argued, even proven beyond a reasonable doubt, that their product is better. Yet they are astounded when they do not make the sale. The problem is that although their product might be better, it may not have as much perceived quality for the customer. Innumerable examples of this phenomenon occur every day. Shampoo manufacturers have discovered that quality is perceived as a function of price; often a higher price on shampoo signifies more quality to customers, even if the product is not better. As another example, one automobile manufacturer uses identical parts when assembling two different brands of cars. This manufacturer's luxury automobile nevertheless is perceived as having more quality, even though both brands of cars have the same parts and components. Or, when it is evaluated using objective criteria and standardized test methods, a window may easily outperform a popular brand, but the popular brand still is perceived as having more quality. Thus, we can say that quality is not a function of objective evaluation.

Product quality is defined quite differently depending on the audience to whom you are speaking. Salespeople invest significant time presenting product features and benefits to customers without linking the importance of those features to their customers. They have not listened to what the customers consider important. A builder may be most concerned with product durability and installation simplicity, while a consumer is more focused on the product's long-term maintenance records. One dealer may value product performance, while another values installation simplicity. The critical issue to recognize is that product quality is only as valuable to any businessperson as the profits that product can generate. To satisfactorily sell a quality profit model, you must listen carefully to discover how your customers feel about quality.

You are quite aware that *service* is an important part of the sales equation. Thus, you may behave like the many salespeople who make vapid boasts regarding the outstanding service their company offers. They assure builders, contractors, and remodelers that they are prepared to do "whatever it takes" to satisfy their customers' wants and needs. They often make these outlandish claims with little consideration for the implications. Too frequently, the result of such claims is that builders either view them with skepticism, or, worse, they strive to take full advantage of the overzealous promises. Then, when they later discover that the salespeople are unable to fulfill the promises they made during the heat of the sales process, the risk of the business relationship deteriorating might already be significant. As with all the other models, the secrets to selling the service profit model are twofold: First, you must understand customers' expectations. Then, second, you must avoid overselling the service you can provide.

When I ask salespeople what they need to know to sell to their prospects, a frequent response includes this statement: "I would like to know what expectations they have of a perfect supplier." I respect the intention, but I feel compelled to understand the reasoning behind the question. Salespeople state that they want to understand what prospects considers "perfect" in a supplier, so they can become that supplier. The problem is, there is no such thing as a perfect supplier. The vision is self-defeating because it raises levels of expectations to an unattainable height. Salespeople must seek to keep everyone's vision based in reality.

Because they recognize that bold promises of service perfection sound trite and unimaginative, some salespeople strive to take the higher road by promising an even higher level of customer service, the vaunted *value-added* profit model. *Value-added* has become a term salespeople commonly use as a means to signify their awareness that they offer a *product plus services* to the customer. When asked what value-added means, however, salespeople quickly respond that they offer things such as great truck drivers and excellent delivery service. They further claim that they provide excellent products, selecting only the highest quality available within the industry. They finally promise that their employer offers the finest after-sale field service available in the marketplace. When the builder reacts nonchalantly or with skepticism to these commonplace boasts, the salesperson fearfully worries that interest is heading in the wrong direction. The key is to actually provide value, not merely talk about it.

Many sales people and organizations within our industry endeavor to build partnerships with their customers. Perhaps you are among the salespeople in your field who strive to forge past the rank of a value-added supplier into the realm of *partner.* An interesting phenomenon is that suppliers usually use the word partnership and their customers use it much less frequently.

When I was attending a promotional training event sponsored by a manufacturer of roofing materials, the host speaker continued to stress the importance of partnerships the manufacturer had with its "partners," many of whom were represented at the seminar. The word *customer* had apparently not been uttered during the entire first day of the event, a situation to which I inadvertently had contributed. Early in the second day of the event, one of the host representatives referred to the seminar participants as "customers."

One participant suddenly interrupted the representative's presentation to say "Hey! Wait a minute. I want to thank you. I've been sitting here for a day and a half. Since I've been here, you are the first person I've heard who called me a customer. I'd like to thank you for that. I ain't your partner. Everybody here keeps calling us partners. When my business struggles and things go bad, you guys ain't gonna be there to offer me money, or financial terms, or assistance of any kind. In fact, your accounts-receivable guy will be on the phone with me within 15 minutes of a late payment. So we are obviously not your partner. I'm a customer, and I thank you for saying so."

The truth is that some customers really do value a partnership relationship, while others want to keep some distance. Some customers value the personal touch, while others are strictly business. Some customers have unrealistic service expectations, while others require only minimal attention. All of the profit models listed above can provide benefit to your customers. The problem lies not in the theory behind the models, but in the presentation of the benefits. Problems result when salespeople's claims begin to sound trite and rehearsed. If you can actually provide profits in some of the ways the different profit models suggest, then you are well on your way to a leadership role in sales within the industry. The reality is that most salespeople have poorly developed skills when it comes to generating profits for their customers.

As an example, consider a salesperson I once coached in a midwestern market. During our three days of travel, he frequently talked about the "partnership" between his employer, a dealer of roofing materials, and his customers, roofing installers. I silently observed as he used the term *partnership* many times during sales presentations. His comments frequently were met with indifference. When I asked him privately what he felt constituted the partnership of which he spoke, he defensively stated that the manufacturers he represented have great literature, leads, and excellent brand awareness.

I persisted by asking him how he thought those characteristics constituted a partnership. He grew quiet and thoughtful. I reminded him that many of his competitors offered the same marketing tools, and then I asked, "Does that make them successful business partners?" He was a talented young salesperson who was eager to grow. He decided that he really didn't know what made him a partner to his customers. When I asked why he used the term, he responded sheepishly that he had heard "other salespeople in the company talk about partnerships with customers, and it sounded good." I asked him whether he wanted some ideas about how to *actually* partner with his customers. He instantly said, "Yes!"

I suggested that we invest any free time we had during the remainder of our travels together searching for builders who would be interested in his products. I promised him that, if we found one or two, we could introduce them to the salespeople at one of his installer's offices. The very next sales call resulted in a lead. We found a builder who believed he had received poor service from his current installer (the subject of price did not come up in the conversation!). When we took that information to one of the young man's installers, the owner of the business was thrilled. He said that he had never received a lead like that from a salesperson—a sad statement on the state of our profession.

The salesperson I was working with was simply elated. Instead of begging his customer to believe how wonderful his company was, he simply demonstrated his ability to generate profits by sharing a valuable lead. As we left the dealer's parking lot in the salesperson's car, he asked whether he should have talked about "partnering" with the customer after he had shared the lead. I asked him whether he thought it was more important to talk about it or actually do it. His smile gave us both the answer I was looking for.

In the end, you probably sell many facets of your company and yourself—products, price, value, service, relationships, expertise, and more. The key to success is to do more than *talk* about profit models. *The key is to actually understand how your customers generate profits.* When you understand how your customers generate profits, only then are you in a position to enhance their business model. More importantly, you will discover that you have much more to offer your customers than competitive pricing. The strategies in this book will help you discover ways to become part of your customer's profit model.

The Supplier's Vision—Profit

The single most important objective of salespeople should be to generate profitable sales for the supplier. I intentionally avoid the term *employer* here to emphasize the independent relationship that exists between the supplier and the salesperson. In some situations, the salesperson is, by contractual agreement, an independent sales agent for a supplier; the salesperson is compensated solely for performance and is responsible for his or her own expenses. In other situations, the salesperson is an employee of the supplier. Regardless of the nature of the relationship, the motive for any salesperson should be to produce profitable sales for the supplier. This goal would seem so obvious that it need not be stated. It does need to be stated, however, because salespeople often focus purely on sales volume and ignore the profitability of a sale.

Surprisingly, many salespeople do not understand how the supplier generates profits. They commonly confuse the definitions of *gross margin* and *markup*. The confusion is costly to suppliers who fail to properly educate their sales staff. Here is an example to test your knowledge and clarify the issue.

If you buy a product from a manufacturer for $100 and resell that product to your customer for $125, what is the gross margin and markup? Many salespeople are confused and mistakenly suppose that the gross margin on this sale is 25 percent. In fact, the gross margin on this sale is 20 percent, while the markup is 25 percent. Confusion about these terms represents a huge error that results in the loss of millions of dollars in profits to suppliers throughout the country. Most suppliers operate their businesses on the foundation of gross-margin dollars, yet what this means remains a surprise to most salespeople. Study Figure 2.3 until you are comfortable with the calculations. If you are unable to understand the calculations, then take an extra moment to review the methods. (As a final test of your understanding, review the simplistic mock financial statement in Figure 2.1 and determine the gross margin for that business. You should recognize that the gross margin in that example is 22 percent.)

A salesperson who miscalculates prices can jeopardize the profitability of the entire organization. If you're like many readers, the relationship between markup and gross margin is probably a simplistic concept you mastered many years ago. If you're like other readers, this might be your first exposure to one of the most critical issues in the industry. Whether you work

FIGURE 2.3 The Impact of Gross Margin and Gross Markup on the Bottom Line

To properly calculate the gross margin, use the following formula:

Selling price = Cost of goods/(1 - Gross Margin)

Example:

- Target gross margin = 25%
- Cost of goods = $6,600
- Selling price = $6,600/(1 - .25)
  = $6,600/.75
  = $8,800

The common misperception is that the gross margin is calculated by multiplying the cost of goods by the gross margin and adding that margin to the total cost of materials. Instead, this is the method for calculating markup.

Selling price = Cost of goods x (1 + Markup)

Example:

- Markup = 25%
- Cost of goods = $6,600
- Selling price = $6,600 x 1.25
  = $8,250

As you can see, the difference between a product's markup and gross margin is significant and takes on huge proportions if you magnify the impact. Depending on the methods by which it calculates markups, the financial statements for an organization that sells $10 million annually will look very different, as the following examples demonstrate,

Markup Model (25% Markup)

Total Revenue =	$10.0 Million
Cost of Goods =	$ 8.0 Million
Net Operating Revenue	$ 2.0 Million

Gross Margin Model (25% Gross Margin)

Total Revenue =	$10.0 Million
Cost of Goods =	$ 7.5 Million
Net Operating Revenue	$ 2.5 Million

The difference between the 25% markup and 25% gross margin results in $500,000 in net operating income! A salesperson that fails to recognize the importance of methods by which suppliers calculate price structures can destroy a supplier's profitability.

FIGURE 2.4 The Difference between Gross Margin and Markup

Cost of Goods	Selling Price	Gross Margin	Markup
$90	$100	10%	11.1%
$88	$100	12%	13.5%
$85	$100	15%	17.6%
$80	$100	20%	25.0%
$75	$100	25%	33.3%
$70	$100	30%	42.9%
$65	$100	35%	53.8%

The *markup* of a product and its *gross margin revenue* are very different to a supplier. Study the table in Figure 2.4 until you can see the difference between the two.

for a dealer, a lumberyard, a two-step distributor, or a manufacturer, you should consider your mastery of this concept a prerequisite for sales success.

The methods by which the supplier generates revenue and profits remain a mystery to many salespeople in the industry. To solve this mystery, many progressive organizations throughout the world are beginning to share the details of their financial statements with employees. But this practice remains an exception rather than the rule, which is a shame because the important issue of profit creation is so misunderstood. Many veteran salespeople are embarrassed to discover that they never understood the proper methods by which margins are calculated. Even if you are not fully aware of the under-lying cost of the materials you sell, keep in mind that the financial success by which your supplier operates is often a matter of only a few percentage points. In this context, your responsibility is to ensure the profitability of each sale you create. The strategies and tactics in the second section of this book are structured to help you as the salesperson maximize the value of your suppliers, thus ensuring maximum opportunity for their profits and your income.

The Salesperson's Vision—Happiness

An important component of your sales success begins with understanding your own motivations and desires. The foundation of one's motivations might not be as obvious as you think. I have interviewed hundreds of sales-people and discovered that their career objectives differ significantly. When they are asked what they are seeking in their sales careers, however, their answers generally fall into one or more of these common categories:

- Money
- Career promotions
- Security
- Growth

Many salespeople will tell you that they are solely seeking ways to make money as quickly as they can. If you were to ask these salespeople what they are seeking during the sales process, they may likely say that they simply want to make the sale: "Show me the money!" Although the ultimate purpose of the job is obviously the pursuit of income, this approach hardly inspires customers to take action. These selfish motivations are transparent and quickly reveal themselves to customers. In fact, this shallow sort of motivation creates animosity between customers and salespeople. The most successful salespeople are usually motivated by goals much loftier than the mere pursuit of coin. What's more, it has been demonstrated time and time again that money does not buy happiness.

Of course, we need money to live, and lack of money jeopardizes our feeling of security. There is nothing wrong with wanting security; unfortunately, many salespeople do not understand how to develop career security. Loyal customers, large salaries, and promotions are mere substitutes for security and happiness. Security is not something that another person can provide. Security is not something that comes from money. Nor is it something that is provided by material wealth.

Security results only from confidence in one's ability to achieve the result, not the result itself. It's been said often enough: "Give the man a fish, and you have fed him for a day. Teach him how to fish, and you have fed him for a lifetime." Sales volume is the fish. The ability to create sales volume and loyal customers is the *ability* to fish. Security comes from a form of motivation found in only the most accomplished salespeople—the pursuit of *personal growth* and the development of ability.

Nearly all salespeople would agree that they would rather build a solid base of customers than have those customers handed to them. If you are given a network of customers, you have a guaranteed source of income for the short term. If you have the ability to create your own network of loyal customers, then you have a guaranteed source of income for the long haul. The difference between your short-term and long-term sales success is therefore predicated not on external factors, but on your internal motivations and skills. To achieve the highest levels of sales skills, salespeople need to recognize the constant need for growth. As Mahatma Gandhi said, "Live as though you will die tomorrow. Learn as though you will live forever."

If you have a solid base of customers, whether you created that base or an employer handed it to you, you are in a different position than a salesperson who is in the process of building a customer base. The difference between the ability to open new accounts and that required to service existing customer accounts has become known as *hunting* versus *farming* in many sales circles. Hunting is perceived as the ability to prospect and open new accounts, whereas farming is perceived as the practice of maintaining relationships with existing accounts. In fact, many organizations have begun to divide the tasks of hunting and farming between separate sales forces. Many sales managers believe the traits that differentiate hunters and farmers are innate. This belief system is disappointing; it means managers assume salespeople cannot be taught these valuable sales skills, particularly the ability to hunt.

Sales leaders recognize that the abilities to hunt and farm *both* are required skill sets to be a successful salesperson in the building industry. All salespeople should pursue the personal growth that makes them adept at both of these important skills. The strategies and tactics included in later chapters employ the use of both hunting and farming sales skills. These skills are not independent of each other; rather, they are complementary subsets of the total set of sales skills.

Hunting sales skills include the tasks that allow one to locate new customers and close deals. Farming sales skills include the tasks that allow one to implement programs and strengthen existing relationships. If salespeople can open new customers but manage those relationships poorly, then the suffering of want will plague them persistently because they will constantly need to find new customers. If salespeople can cultivate existing relationships but are unable to open new opportunities, then they will quickly discover that their credibility suffers, and the suffering of want will persist. The only way to achieve security and happiness is to develop sales skills that are inclusive of hunting and farming.

The only way to achieve security and happiness is to develop sales skills that are inclusive of hunting and farming.

Security results from knowing you are able to accomplish the tasks of a job under any circumstances. Security eliminates suffering. Security provides happiness. Thus, true happiness results from confidence in your own skills.

Behaviors and Values

It is not what we know that counts. It is what we do with what we know. And it is not what we *think* we do—it is what we *actually* do. The problem facing many salespeople is that they fail to objectively evaluate their own performance. This problem results from a detachment between their stated values and their behaviors. To develop strategic sales skills, salespeople must fully understand the difference between values and behaviors.

A *value* is a stated belief; a *behavior* is the action a person takes. The reality of our society and our world is that our stated values do not always match our behaviors. I refer to this point frequently in later chapters. Human beings by nature are more capable of boasting about their personal beliefs than actually mirroring those values with their behavior. This topic is important for any salesperson sincerely interested in the pursuit of personal growth.

An individual challenge we all face is the internal battle of pride versus humility. Ben Franklin once listed 12 characteristics that he vowed to cultivate in his lifetime. He happily pursued this goal throughout his life. What was remarkable about Ben Franklin was that he strived constantly for personal growth and betterment of his character. That type of dedication to self-improvement and self-honesty are rare in today's world. Ben was able to select values and characteristics he believed were important, and then he cultivated the behaviors that aligned with those values. When he discovered that his values and behaviors were inconsistent, he strived to change his behaviors. Ben's persistent approach to self-improvement allowed him to become one of the great Americans in history.

You may wonder why this information is important to you. If you are like most salespeople, you are continually striving to avoid price concessions and other challenges, all of which create fear. If someone were to ask you whether you consider yourself a salesperson who relies on price, would you immediately defend your character by asserting that the "other salespeople are price salespeople"? My experience is that a large majority of salespeople assert that it is the other guy who acts on price alone.

A New Vision—Strategic Selling

If you were to ask most salespeople whether they consciously focus on helping their customers and suppliers become more profitable, they would probably tell you that this is their number-one objective. As we've discussed, the reality is that many salespeople behave fearfully and selfishly, failing to realize that they should focus on helping other people eliminate their own fears. If you are experiencing the fear and suffering that plague many salespeople, consider changing your vision. Focus on helping other people achieve their goals and dreams.

Strategic selling skills will help you strengthen your alignment of values and behaviors. They will help you overcome the fear of relying on price competitiveness. They will provide benchmarks from which you can manage your own behaviors effectively, constantly improving your selling skills and generating immense personal growth in your career. Strategic selling skills will make you a happier and more optimistic salesperson.

CHAPTER THREE

STRATEGIES
FOR SALES SUCCESS

As a salesperson, to view your sales successes and failures in all-or-nothing terms is natural. If you make the sale, you win and you are happy. If you lose the sale, you are defeated and you suffer. The problem with win-lose thinking is that every activity in the process becomes meaningless if the only measure of success is the completion of a sale. The time between meetings and proposals is then plagued with pessimism. Any minor success in the process, such as a great presentation, becomes meaningless because you cannot attach a victory to the outcome. Your profession becomes an emotional roller coaster on which either happiness or sadness is the outcome of every sale. You lose the joy of your effort.

Instead, rather than expecting to succeed at all times, expect frequent failure. A baseball player knows that he will fail more often than he succeeds. A fisherman will often wait many hours before landing a catch. A soccer team can win the World Cup even though it fails to score for 89 minutes and 59 seconds of a 90-minute match. Athletes recognize that success will occur if they repeat the right habits and actions frequently enough. In spite of predictable failures, they measure their success as a percentage rather than in all-or-nothing terms.

Fortunately, there are strategies to alleviate the suffering of win-lose thinking. These strategies will provide you happiness and (ironically) more wins in your career. Sales strategies let you replace the win-lose mentality with intermediate goals and secondary objectives that can support your bigger objective, which is to fulfill an acceptable percentage of your sales opportunities.

A *strategy* is merely a game plan that guides you to the accomplishment of an objective. In some ways, a strategy is similar to a value, in that neither are actions, but both can provide guidelines for human behaviors. Many salespeople enter the field of battle equipped with no strategic game plan; thus, their behaviors become random reactions to the activities of customers, suppliers, coworkers, and industry pressure. With strategic selling, you can proactively align your actions and behaviors with an unambiguous vision.

A *tactic* is an action that can support and fulfill your strategy. Although a particular tactic may seem appropriate, even necessary, it may fail to support the strategy. For example, a common sales tactic is to eagerly mail literature and technical data to prospective customers, in the hope that a meeting will ensue because of the interest the information generates. After they receive the information, however, the prospects might conclude that they have no interest in the product and, therefore, no interest in a meeting. The tactic did not generate the necessity for a meeting.

In the above example, the tactic is not necessarily a "bad" one. Stand-alone tactics should not be judged as good or bad, positive or negative. Tactics should be judged as choices among alternative actions. Unfortunately, many salespeople fail to consciously associate their tactics with corresponding strategies. The tactic of mailing information might accomplish the desired strategy 10 percent of the time. Another tactic might be to telephone prospects in hope of scheduling meetings. Or you might discover that telemarketing results in scheduling an appointment 20 percent of the time. Compared to the mass mailing, you would conclude that the telephone call is a more effective tactic to satisfy your strategy of getting a meeting. Determining which tactics best support your strategies can be accomplished only if you measure the results.

Suppose, for example, that you are a very organized salesperson, and you successfully measured the results from our previous example. You might discover that the prospects with whom you met as a result of the direct mailer were far more interested than those you contacted by telephone. Although you might have concluded that more meetings resulted from the tactic of telemarketing, you discovered that in fact you sold a higher percentage of prospects who first received brochures in the mail. You discovered that 7 percent of all direct-mail prospects eventually became customers, while you achieved sales success with only 4 percent of all prospects from your telemarketing efforts. In this example, you would accurately conclude that the direct-mail method was the superior prospecting method. And so you might replace your former strategy of "getting an appointment" with a more sophisticated strategy of "getting an appointment with a pre-qualified prospect."

The reality is that most salespeople do not have the inclination or the resources to measure the results of their behavior to this degree. The good news is that such measurement is not a necessary aspect of strategic selling. The most critical aspect of strategic selling is that you create a plan and employ tactics that support the plan. You will discover that your instincts provide significant insights and guide the process of improving your strategic planning and tactical execution.

> The most critical aspect of strategic selling is that you create a plan and employ tactics that support the plan.

The concept of strategic selling may seem daunting at the outset. Although you may not feel equipped to plan successful sales strategies, you will be pleased to discover that most successful strategies are simple. In everyday life, children and everyday Joes frequently design and implement strategies.

We all have seen children manipulate adults with the efficiency of a surgeon. A child who wants his parents to take him to the zoo will cry, cajole, hug, adore, and offer affection to accomplish his strategy. The strategy is the trip to the zoo. The tactics are the temper tantrums and promises of affection. A clever spouse may secretly desire to dine at a nice restaurant rather than cook dinner. To accomplish the strategy, the spouse may employ any number of tactics. In some cases, it may take only one. For example, he may offer to whip up a quick spam casserole. His wife, quickly envisioning the agony of ingesting the unappetizing meal, will immediately offer to take her spouse to a nice restaurant. Mission accomplished!

The point is that strategies give you a purpose for your actions. They provide guidelines by which you can become more objective about the outcomes of your behaviors. Personal growth results when you continually improve your behavior and the results of your sales activity. Strategic selling allows you to clarify your vision and become more objective in the evaluation of your results. With strategic selling, instead of reacting negatively to challenging situations, you become objective in your evaluations and, more importantly, aware of alternative actions that you can take.

Microsales versus Macrosales

In the field of economics, theories are divided into two disciplines—*microeconomics* and *macroeconomics*. Microeconomics is the study of individual business operations, while macroeconomics is the study of national and international economies. We can divide the theories and practices of selling into two different disciplines as well: *microsales* and *macrosales*.

Microsales theory focuses on the one-on-one relationship between the supplier and the customer. Microsales strategies are therefore focused on the plans and actions that increase your sales success with individual customers and prospects. Microsales issues focus on planning individual meetings, developing questioning skills and presentation skills, and numerous other issues related to creating a single successful relationship with a customer.

Macrosales theory focuses on managing the bigger picture. Macrosales strategies focus on the activities that allow you to plan entire weeks, months, and years of activity. Macrosales issues focus on measuring sales potential, setting goals, improving administrative skills, and other issues related to long-term sales success.

To successfully develop both microsales and macrosales strategies, you must first understand the market opportunity. The most important strategy for every salesperson is to *maximize the value of the opportunity in the market*. And although a shotgun approach might work adequately, much more security and happiness are likely in a methodical approach that inspires confidence in the future. Thus, your microsales skills are the laser tactics that let you manage the macrosales opportunity within your market.

> The most important strategy for every salesperson is to *maximize the value of the opportunity in the market.*

A Box of Diamonds

Your performance as a salesperson in a territory of limited prospects is no different from that of a gemologist who examines the potential value of a box of jewels.

As the information in Figure 3.1 demonstrates, every gem presents a value opportunity that the expert objectively appraises without emotion. For example, a gemologist would not dispose of a five-carat emerald in favor of a miniscule diamond. The emerald, although perhaps not the gemologist's favorite jewel, nevertheless provides a much better value opportunity.

As a salesperson, you are presented with a box of limited resources in the form of your territory. Your success is based on your ability to objectively evaluate and capitalize on all of the opportunities in your market. You have many gems to examine, ranging from builders who produce hundreds of homes annually to one-person operations that produce only a few houses per year. And there are more: remodelers, architects, dealers, lumberyards, trade contractors, general contractors, installers, and do-it-yourselfers. Every potential customer in your market is a gem worthy of examination.

If you are anything like the majority of salespeople in your market, then you probably have focused your sales effort on a narrow target audience. Many salespeople are adept at capitalizing on obvious opportunities. However, it is apparent that they ignore many valuable gems. The best proof of this comes from the salespeople themselves. They shamelessly admit investing almost no time calling on architects. In countless seminars in which roofing and siding salespeople were present, these attendees happily stated that

FIGURE 3.1 Evaluate Market Opportunities

A study of the diamond business provides an illustrative example of how important it is for salespeople to evaluate all the opportunities available in their market. For example, you may know a little bit about the diamond business. If you have ever purchased a diamond, you probably learned about the Four Cs—color, cut, clarity and carat. The Four Cs of the diamond business are the criteria by which jewelers evaluate the individual value of the diamonds. Thus, the formula by which the value of a diamond is established, in which V equals the value and c represents color, cut, clarity, and carat, is

$$V = c + c + c + c$$

Most people do not know that the DeBeers family, owners of approximately 90 percent of the world's natural diamond resources, are not welcomed visitors to the United States of America. They have been able to establish monopolistic control over the world-wide distribution of diamonds. The power of their monopoly makes them subject to legal actions in the United States, which explains why their North American meetings are held in Toronto, Canada. We'll leave the methods by which the DeBeers family distribute the diamonds to the concerns of US trade regulators, the power of this monopoly provides a lesson from which we can learn more about our own business behavior.

The delivery of diamonds begins with shipments of boxes loaded with the precious gems to distributors located throughout the world. The distributors are subject to contractual agreements that require them to wire millions of dollars in payment *before* they receive their diamond shipment, and so they are denied any credit terms. The weight of the materials determines the price they pay, and so they are denied opportunities for negotiation. The distributors have no choice regarding the selection of gems they will receive, and so they are denied the opportunity to shop for product quality.

If you were a diamond distributor under these circumstances and had just paid millions of dollars for a box of rocks, you would meticulously examine each of those rocks to ensure a maximum return on your investment. You would certainly evaluate the worth of each gem, one at a time, to ensure that you miss no opportunities for profit. Your success as a diamond dealer would be contingent upon the ability to achieve the maximum return on investment.

they sell exclusively to installers of material, while they ignore their customers' customers—the builders. Manufacturer sales representatives openly concede that they invest nearly all of their sales effort in the offices of dealers, with purchasing agents and managers, while they ignore the secondary audience of builders, remodelers, and architects.

You would not think twice about choosing between a $25,000 account and a $100,000 customer who provides loyalty, fair margins, and long-term growth potential. Every salesperson in the world would state that the latter customer is the more profitable customer. Yet why do roofing and siding salespeople persistently call on the $25,000 installer, while they completely ignore the $100,000 builder? Why do manufacturer sales representatives invest their time during their territory "milk run" visiting the $25,000 dealer and ignore the $100,000 architect? The answer to these questions can only be prejudice or ignorance. These people must not know that these other gems are waiting in their box of rocks!

Likewise, just as a gemologist evaluates the quality of precious jewels, it is a wise practice for a salesperson to evaluate the quality of precious prospects. Quality evaluation is an essential tactic that supports the strategy of maximizing market opportunity. My day of travel during a coaching session with a 14-year veteran of sales is depicted in Figure 3.2. This salesperson's activity epitomized the challenge that faces all salespeople in the industry—time and territory management. The letters represent the quality of prospects, in which A is the ideal prospect/customer, B is a good prospect/customer and C represents a poor prospect/customer.

Figure 3.2 is an accurate representation of our travel. We met at the salesperson's home office and visited seven prospects and customers during the day. The arrows represent the direction and order of our meetings, and the squiggly line in the southeast corner of the territory represents the half hour of driving time during which we were lost. The salesperson had no area map and never called for directions at any point. We were in his sports-utility vehicle for nearly five hours and in front of prospects and customers for less than one hour total. The only appointment the salesperson had scheduled was the first sales call, represented by the boxed letter A. Not surprisingly, this appointment was our most productive sales call of the day.

Several conclusions become evident as you inspect the map. We drove relentlessly and aimlessly, logging nearly 200 miles in one day. We could have accomplished as much in only a few hours had we concentrated our efforts in just one section of his territory. He had done little prior planning for our day together. I suspect that many of this particular salesperson's days went unplanned. Because he lacked a clear vision or strategy, the quality of the customers and prospects he visited also was poor.

That this salesperson could dramatically improve his performance is obvious. Lacking any form of strategy, he drove aimlessly, with no clear expectations. He was obviously hoping something positive would emerge from random efforts. Such an approach often provides marginal success, but it is hardly enough to achieve personal happiness and dazzling success in a career. It is important to realize that many salespeople behave in this same way, repeating poor performances daily.

The critical point to make from this example is that having the proper territory and using good time management can help maximize

FIGURE 3.2 Poor Territory Management

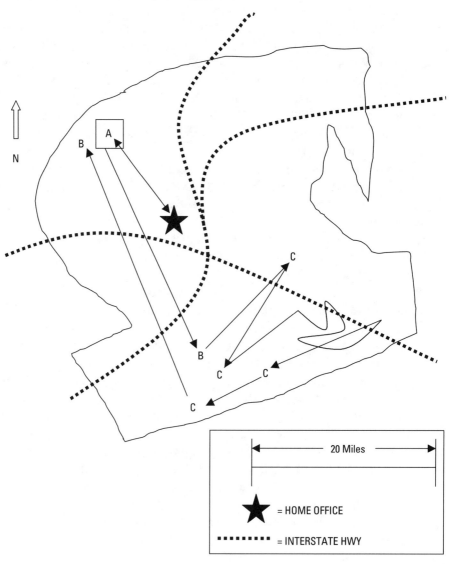

your microsales efforts and the market opportunity. This salesperson traversed back and forth through his territory with an insistent belief that he should focus his efforts on a specific category of builder. He ignored remodelers, installers, and architects completely. His territory includes a large geographic field in which his target builders are sparsely distributed, similar to the vision depicted in Figure 3.3. This view of the territory underestimates the abundance of available opportunity.

Having the proper territory and using good time management can help maximize your microsales efforts and the market opportunity.

FIGURE 3.3 Ineffective Territory Overview

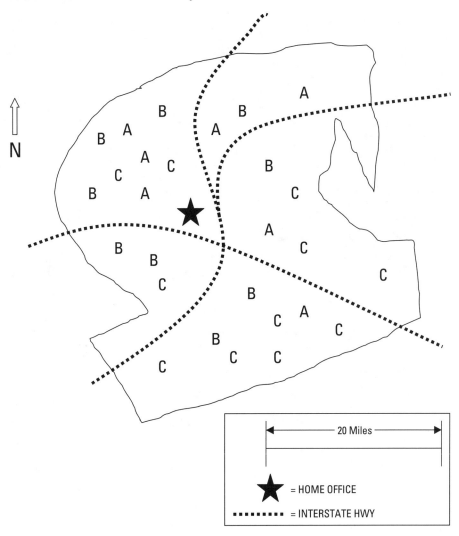

Strategically focused salespeople will see their territories as mine fields abundantly stocked with a variety of potential gems. Those who recognize the abundance of their territories can eliminate their win-lose fear and resulting suffering. If the sales veteran I traveled with were to view his same territory from a more inclusive perspective, it would resemble Figure 3.4. This view of the territory doubles his sales opportunity. By dividing the territory into manageable zones (as outlined by the heavy dashed lines), he would further discover that he could dramatically increase his efficiency. Were the salesperson I coached to reevaluate and reorganize his territory, he would clearly see that our day together could have been much more productive. He could have accomplished more in two or three hours than he accomplished in that entire day.

FIGURE 3.4 Effective Territory Overview

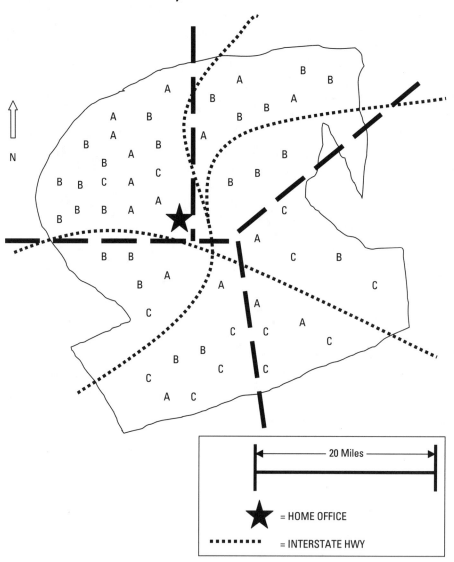

N

20 Miles

★ = HOME OFFICE

•••••••• = INTERSTATE HWY

The obvious obstacle to this new approach is the challenge of selling to a variety of audiences—e.g., architects, remodelers, builders, and dealers. We would consider a gemologist foolish were he to ignore valuable rubies and emeralds solely because his expertise is diamonds. We would recommend that he learn how to evaluate and cut other gems, to maximize his business opportunity. Similarly, manufacturer sales representatives typically concentrate on dealers of materials because their expertise is with those "customers." Dealer salespeople concentrate on builders because their expertise is with those "customers." Window replacement salespeople (and siding, roofing, and other salespeople of remodeling products) concentrate on remodelers because their expertise is with those "customers." Almost nobody invests time with architects because they "don't spend money with you anyway." But the reality is that salespeople are ignoring valuable gems that are right under their noses as a result of such ignorance or prejudice.

If you view your territory as what you see in Figure 3.4, you will instantly recognize the abundance of opportunities that are being overlooked. Moreover, you will discover that you become far less focused on the type of prospect (i.e., emerald or diamond, builder or remodeler) and more focused on the *value* of each microsales opportunity.

If the Four Cs—color, cut, clarity, and carat—allow the diamond merchant to evaluate the potential worth of his gems, then, you might ask, what are the criteria by which you can evaluate your potential customers? Some of the characteristics you may use to evaluate the ideal customer include high sales volume, high gross margin, loyalty, long-term sales potential, and so forth. In other words, not all prospects are created equal. By assessing the potential value (V) of each "gem" in your territory, you will wisely allocate your time with the most profitable opportunities. If (v) = sales volume, (g) = gross margin, (l) = loyalty, (t) = long-term potential, and (p) = the expected use of your product, you can calculate the potential value of an account using the following equation:

$$V = v + g + l + t + p$$

You might appropriately give more weight to a specific component characteristic. You might value long-term potential more highly than the volume of a one-time project sale. You can properly reason that $50,000 in annual sales repeated over a 10-year period is more valuable than a one-time sale of $175,000. You might value, based upon your personal compensation package, the gross margin value of an account more than the overall sales volume. Regardless of the basis for your measurements, you can objectively evaluate the potential value of all your prospects or customers. Whether the prospect is a builder, an architect, a dealer, an installer, a remodeler, a general contractor, or a woman working from the basement of her home, as an interior designer should not matter. Remember, your market has many rough gems waiting to be polished and turned into priceless jewels.

Sales Roles and Four Target Audiences

The complexities of our distribution channels and the constantly changing industry terminology create confusion that must be resolved to structure effective sales strategies. For practical application, I have reduced target audiences into four distinct categories: builder, architect, dealer, and salesperson. With the exception of consumers, every business entity conveniently fits into one of these simplistic categories.

Four Categories of the Target Customer

1. **Builder**—This category includes all industry professionals who purchase and install products. The category includes homebuilders, remodelers, general contractors, developers, subcontractors, and installers.

2. **Architect**—This category includes industry professionals who provide technical design influence, such as architects, building designers, interior designers, and engineers.

3. **Dealer**—This broad category includes all businesses that sell materials to the builder category. This category includes lumberyards, wholesale distributors, one-step distributors, two-step distributors, retailers, big-box retailers, and the like. The primary audience of this category is the *sales leadership personnel* of the dealer.

4. **Salesperson**—In general, the objective with this audience is to farm within the customer account to grow the business. The audience of people within this category may be more definable than one would expect. The primary audience of this category includes your *customers' salespeople.*

When you read the sections related to Builder sales, the strategies and tactics apply to home builders, remodelers, general contractors, developers, trade contractors, and installers. The builder audience purchases materials to be installed for the builder's customers. You may need to consider subtle adjustments of the tactics for each subgroup. Nevertheless, you will discover that all varieties of builder types share common characteristics. The different builder types usually employ similar tactics when they are negotiating with their suppliers.

The category titled Architect applies to architects, building designers, interior designers, and engineers. You will discover that these audiences, although usually not directly involved in the purchase of products, share the common characteristic that they frequently influence product selections. The single most difficult challenge for salespeople is determining to what small segment of this target audience they should allocate their time. Many architects will not have dramatic influence, while others will strongly influence the product-selection process. The key to success with this group is to determine which jewels will reap the most abundant rewards.

The third target audience for whom strategies and tactics will be discussed is the Dealer. The Dealer audience includes a variety of types such as lumberyards, wholesale distributors, one-step distributors, two-step distributors, retailers, big-box retailers, and any other organizations that purchase materials from a supplier and then resell them to a builder.

Before we can fully capitalize on the opportunity available with the fourth target audience, we must clarify the sales roles that exist in our industry. Depending on the target audience and situation, salespeople play two different roles in their careers—promotional sales and project sales. As *promotional sales* representatives, salespersons must possess skills that enable them to successfully sell products to other salespeople, who in turn resell the same product. As *project sales* representatives, salespersons' activities should focus on generating immediate transactions.

For example, a manufacturer representative is usually (but not always) in the role of a promotional sales representative. The manufacturer representative typically sells to dealers who resell products. The dealer salespeople are usually (but not always) in the project sales role, generating transactions with builders, remodelers, and installers. The manufacturer representative provides training services as well as promotional support in the form of literature and samples. Problems result when salespeople perceive that they are permanently in either one role or the other. This is why I shun the terms *hunters* and *farmers* introduced in Chapter 2. In reality, salespeople are not hunters *or* farmers; rather, they must be adept at both skills—hunting *and* farming.

Manufacturer representatives involved in sales calls to builders or architects are in a project sales role. Sales to builders are commonly transactional in nature and thus require highly developed project sales skills. If salespeople misconstrue their role in such sales, behaving as promotional sales representatives, they will quickly lose credibility with customers and other salespeople. Conversely, dealer sales representatives who conduct meetings with a small group of their customers' salespeople will lose credibility if they push for instant transactions. During the meeting, customers' salespeople are in no position to place orders because they are not in front of their customers.

TWO ROLES OF INDUSTRY SALESPEOPLE

1. **Promotional Sales**—This sales role defines salespeople engaged in the task of selling to customers who resell products.

2. **Project Sales**—This sales role defines salespeople in the process of selling directly to builders or architects.

Thus, the fourth target audience of Relationship Development includes your customers' salespeople. The complexity of channel distribution creates countless situations in which a salesperson sells customers products that are resold by the customers' salespeople. This situation places the original salesperson in a promotional sales role. Promotional activities are designed to create opportunities for other salespeople to sell your product more effectively. The rewards for successful promotion to other salespeople are immense. Salespeople who can successfully gain sales commitment from their customers' salespeople achieve a status that garners respect, credibility, and loyalty.

FIGURE 3.5 Sales Roles to the Four Target Audiences

Audience	Sale	Sales Role
Builder	Transaction	Project Sales
Architect	Influence	Project Sales
Dealer Leadership	Program Commitment	Promotional Sales
Salesperson	Sales Commitment	Promotional Sales

This is the crux of the message I hope to share in this book: Credibility results from the constant development of sales skills that enable you to successfully sell to any person within the industry. Common perceptions are that sales roles become delineated as shown in Figure 3.5. We know that dealers sell to builders. Debate has raged for years regarding the appropriate location of responsibility for architectural promotion. Because I have no stake in the debate, I will end it now by stating that dealers are responsible for marketing to architects, an assertion that I will develop later in the text. Ultimately, the best salespeople are those who successfully possess both promotional and project sales skills. Salespeople who recognize this truth and cultivate the skills necessary to sell to every audience in our industry discover opportunities for immense personal growth.

Opportunity is when preparation meets luck. If you are prepared to sell to all the audiences within the complex channels of our industry, you will feel your confidence and income soar. To meet this challenge, you must first recognize that your prospects and customers also have business skills. Your customers and prospects employ strategies and tactics to counter your offensive. Before you can develop successful sales strategies, you should investigate the purchasing strategies of your adversaries.

"Adversary" Strategies

The use of a strategy, by definition, assumes that there is an adversary against whom one engages in competition. When you are engaged in the practice of sales with any of the four target audiences, that audience becomes your adversary. At first glance, the term *adversary* may seem too strong, implying that your relationship with customers and prospects is marked by belligerence and hostility. Reality shows us that many of our relationships *are* combative. Were they not so, we would happily discover that price negotiations and service demands would be nonexistent. We in fact know that just the opposite is true: Customers frequently demand competitive pricing, high service levels, and instant answers to difficult questions. Thus, when you are negotiating, presenting, questioning, and servicing your customers or prospects, you should recognize that they are your adversaries.

Volumes have been written on the various personality types that you will encounter. But let's assume for the purposes of simplicity that all of your adversaries are similar in disposition and behavioral styles. In my seminars, I divide the personality types into four purchasing styles—fast, power, friendly, or analytical.

1. The *fast buyer* is the most aggressive type of customer, seeking immediate results.

2. The *power buyer,* also seeking results, is focused on the bigger picture of long-term benefit. Both the power buyer and the friendly buyer are interested in long-term relationships, but the power buyer is more likely to focus on business issues.

3. The *friendly buyer* and the power buyer are both interested in long-term relationships; but the friendly buyer is more interested in personal rapport.

4. The *analytical buyer,* as the name implies, is focused on technical issues related to data, and the scientific analysis of products and services.

A separate text can be written on the subject of personality styles. For the purposes of strategic selling, it is worth noting that your strategic behavior should at least partially consider the personality characteristics of your audience.

The preparation of your sales strategies also must take into consideration the various negotiation techniques that you will encounter. For the sake of simplicity, we will assume that your prospects and customers fall into one of the following three styles of negotiator:

1. *Compromising*—Some of your adversaries will be extremely compromising, relying on mutually beneficial transactions.

2. *Combative*—Others will be more combative, continually focusing on ways to gain a competitive edge in negotiations.

3. *Cooperative*—Some of the more visionary adversaries you will encounter will be very cooperative, striving to build long-term relationships of mutual profit.

If you can recognize your adversaries' fundamental strategies and tactics, you will be prepared to employ countermeasures that result in mutually beneficial relationships and, as always, more happiness.

Builder Strategies

Builders commonly display all three styles of negotiation behavior. The nature of the business relationships between builders and suppliers is transactional in nature. Builders buy products to complete a project. After the project is complete, the relationship theoretically cycles back to the bidding (and negotiation) phases of the selling process. The key to success is to recognize when you are dealing with a combative customer and when you are working with someone who is more compromising.

As a primary negotiation strategy with suppliers, combative builders strive to rush salespeople through the sales process, pushing them to provide prices before quality discussions take place. Combative negotiators request bids from numerous suppliers in order to play one against another. Combative negotiators continue to avoid discussions regarding product and service features. After pressuring salespeople for prices, they routinely pressure for lower prices even when prices may be competitive and fair. The combative builder strives to win in negotiations by obtaining the lowest price possible every time. In this way, builders "speed up" salespeople in the bidding process as a strategy that benefits the builder and potentially hampers the salesperson.

Many builders are much more compromising in their behaviors. They recognize the value, in terms of time, that a loyal, competent supplier can provide. Many builders find it tedious to continually shop each project, hoping to save a few dollars. They view this behavior as penny wise and pound foolish. Instead, the strategy of these builders is to *cultivate a network of quality suppliers*. An obvious selling strategy for salespeople would be to seek out the compromising builder.

There are rare instances in which builders work diligently with suppliers. Their strategy is to *cultivate supplier partnerships that allow the builder to outsell and outmarket their competition*. Tim, the manager of a lumberyard in Chicago, worked with a developer who wanted committed suppliers who offered co-op advertising and special after-sale services.

> The co-op arrangement between suppliers and customers allows each to "cooperatively" participate in advertising and promotional costs toward the mutual benefit for both parties.

Most salespeople would have quickly acquiesced to the demands of this developer without first seeking appropriate remuneration. Tim recognized that these requested services meant added costs, and he clarified his need to charge more to provide those services. In this case, the developer and salesperson worked together to gain market share through cooperative negotiations.

Despite the fact that we know builder audiences differ by personality type, negotiation style, and many other business factors, many salespeople continue to engage in win-lose sales behavior. We frantically seek "project opportunities to bid on" and react submissively to combative negotiators. A Pavlovian conditioned response develops when we begin to instinctively expect price challenges. The result is that we create responses that might not otherwise occur. We must remember that not all builders are created equally. In fact, they represent many gems of different shapes, sizes, and colors.

If we look back at the equation that evaluates each of our customers, the formula for assessing the worthiness of an account can be expanded to include one additional criterion, credit-worthiness. Where c = credit-worthiness, the value of a builder (V_b) becomes the following:

$$V_b = v + g + l + t + p + c$$

Just how important credit-worthiness is to a supplier requires no explanation. A builder cannot become a customer if that builder is without a solid credit history. In fact, it is probably more accurate to visualize credit-worthiness as a logical value rather than a relative value. If builders have no credit, then you probably do not want their business. In other words,

If $c = no$, then the $V_b = 0$.
If $c = yes$, then $V_b = v + g + l + t + p$

Of course there are exceptions. A credit department might take a chance on a new business that holds promise. A customer in difficult circumstances can make COD arrangements. However, generally speaking, bad credit equals bad prospect.

The subtle inclusion of this additional criterion to our equation seems relatively unimportant at this moment. After all, you hardly need to read a book to tell you that credit-worthiness is a non-negotiable consideration. You will soon discover that this quality clarifies the method by which you can value an architect.

Architect Strategies

The most important factors to affect the success of an architectural firm are design aesthetics, project functionality, professional liability, and, of course, profitability. The salesperson's relationship with architects differs from that with builders because profitability to the architect and to the product supplier are not directly linked. Unlike builders, architects bill for their time. Builders generate profits by reducing costs, thus creating pressure to lower prices with suppliers. A sales relationship with an architect therefore provides an opportunity to establish a unique business-to-business relationship, one in which the relationship can focus almost exclusively on cooperative business issues. Although relationships with builders may more often be combative than cooperative, the opposite can be said of those with architects. Whereas builders require lower costs to make profits, architects require readily available information and familiarity with products to allow for the adequate billing of their time and the satisfaction of their clients. Whereas builders apply pressure to ensure a well-structured business relationship, architects apply pressure to ensure a well-structured structure. Pardon the pun, but it is true! Calling on architects can be fun simply because they are focused on fun issues such as product features, product accessories, product options, performance specifications, and installation details—the stuff salespeople like to talk about.

The Benefits of Architectural Sales

---

* Your sale will be easier.

* Your administrative skills will grow exponentially.

* Architects are actually interested in product features.

* You can accomplish a lot in a little time.

* Architects wield influence.

* Architects design your future.

* The best projects are not publicized.

In fact, sales relationships with architects have a number of benefits, including the following:

Your sales will be easier. Your competition usually ignores architects. If you invest time cultivating a relationship with only a few qualified architects in your market, you will have a strong leg up on your competition. From these relationships, you will be referred to builders and other architects in the community. You will soon discover that your sales are increasing and you are getting better prices for your products. These are your rewards for cultivating the gems of opportunity that your competitors have ignored.

Your administrative skills will grow exponentially. One of the extraordinary benefits of architectural sales, when executed properly, is the growth of salespeople's administrative skills. Whereas employers frequently keep detailed records on sales volume, quote activity, and other data relevant to direct accounts, they keep no such records on relationships with architects. Salespeople who are dedicated to the pursuit of architectural sales will develop administrative methods that track project activity, database information, builder referrals, project referrals, and sales to the architects' clients. The development of these administrative skills provides salespeople with the opportunity to enhance their recordkeeping for all their business relationships.

Architects are actually interested in product features. Architects are very visual in their learning methods. After all, they draw pictures for a living. Thus, they are very focused on product features and performance specifications as they relate to design benefit for their clients.

You can accomplish a lot in a little time. Perhaps the largest misconception regarding architectural sales is the time necessary to achieve a satisfactory sales experience. Architects are frequently paid for their time. Thus, they value salespeople who can quickly and efficiently conduct sales meetings. For an entire architectural sales call, including qualifying questions, to last less than 10 minutes is not unusual.

Architects wield influence. This is the big payoff. Architects influence the selection of products, particularly when their clients own the projects.

Architects design your future. For an architect to invest many months designing a single project is not unusual. As a result of their architectural sales efforts, some salespeople have discovered millions of dollars in projects that sit "waiting in the wings." We all know that the earlier we are involved in a project, the more likely we are to sell it. When we are aware of numerous projects that will be coming available for bids, we are in position to sell the projects many months before our competition knows of their existence.

The best projects are not publicized. Many salespeople spend a lifetime reviewing public reports from industry services, newspapers, building permits, lead reports, and other industry data. This method of obtaining leads is so common that competition is intensified. But the types of residential projects designed by architects are generally not publicized. Moreover, these are frequently the grandest projects being built in the market.

An architect is one of the many "rocks" in your box that, if "polished," can provide you profits and happiness in your career. Why so few salespeople take the time to call on these valuable architects astounds me, and to hear their reasons fascinates me. The generalizations I often hear arise from shallow prejudices based on ignorance and conjecture. Some of the strongest opinions about architects come from salespeople who have never called on an architect. Even you, the reader, might have strong opinions about the architectural profession, despite a lack of experience working with this audience.

Salespeople often inaccurately assert that architects "don't know what they're doing," "draw things that can't even be built," and "don't know the 'real world.' " These salespeople falsely believe that architects are not directly influential in the selection of products, somehow imagining that architects write project specifications that are intended as mere guidelines, changeable according to the builder's whim. These prejudicial generalizations are based on a lack of understanding of the architectural profession. The result of these inaccurate generalizations is unrealized income for salespeople.

At the same time, some generalizations about architects are accurate. For example, salespeople can expect that, if they sell an architect on the value of a product, another dealer might get the sale and reap the rewards of their effort.

Salespeople are correct to assume that numerous sales visits are necessary to establish a solid business relationship with an architect. Salespeople are also correct in assuming that some architects are not worthy of a significant time investment. However, every one of these accurate generalizations about architects is also true of builders. Yet these generalizations don't usually prevent salespeople from calling on builders.

These beliefs by others become your opportunity for increased sales, income, credibility, respect, and personal and career happiness. While your competitors continue to wallow in false beliefs and prejudicial opinions, you can snap up the gems of opportunity that they overlook.

You will commonly discover that architects dictate which products will be selected for a particular project. They frequently produce construction documents according to specific product data and thereby select the product for the client. In other situations, architects' influence is inconsequential. The value of an architectural account is largely dependent on the degree of control and influence that the architect wields during the selection of materials.

One single criterion can help you identify the degree of control any particular architect wields. Just like any other business, an architect has customers and clients. The client of a residential architect is either the builder or the owner of the project. When an architect is working for the builder, the builder generally influences product selection. When the architect's client is the owner of the project, sometimes called a *private client,* the architect has a much greater degree of control and influence in the specification process. *Thus, the most important qualifying question you can ask a residential architect is "Who is your usual client—the owner or the builder?"*

When the architect works for his private clients, your payoff as a salesperson is direct influence with the project owner, the ultimate decision-maker. This relationship is the single most important difference between an architect and a builder. The architect "pays" you with referrals and favorable bid opportunities, whereas the builder writes a check. Architects will provide revenue and sales even though they will rarely spend money with you as the supplier.

Remember our equation about the valuation of builders. We can replace (c), the credit-worthiness of a builder, with (o), where (o) is the owner's involvement with the architect. In this way, the value of the architect (V_a) can be calculated as follows:

$$V_a = v + g + l + t + p + o$$

If the residential architect does not wield influence with the project owner, then the value of that architectural account may be severely diminished. You will discover exceptions as you develop your architectural sales skills. I make this point with great respect to all architects and the hope that no salesperson would ever deny any architect the information necessary to complete a project design.

I have discovered that salespeople quickly become frustrated with architectural sales, primarily because they are chasing bad clients. Err on the side of conservatism, particularly if you have never called on architects before, and begin your architectural sales career by focusing on those architects whom you *know* to be influential in the product-purchasing process. As you cultivate your skills, you will discover that architectural influence is a matter of degree.

Thus, to get started in architectural sales, visualize the following:

$$If\ o\ (owner\ as\ the\ client\ of\ the\ architect) = no,\ then\ the\ V_b = 0^*.$$
$$If\ o = yes,\ then\ V_a = v + g + l + t + p$$

Later, you will discover that architectural influence is a relative value and return to the proper visualization:

$$V_a = v + g + l + t + p + o$$

The formulas in this chapter may seem overly theoretical to many salespeople who prefer to boast of their ability to fly by the seat of their pants. However, large corporations commonly use these formulas to establish the value of individual customers. Airlines rate and reward customers based upon the frequency of their patronage. Grocery stores commonly track the spending habits of their shoppers via discount "value cards." The leasing division of one the world's largest corporations regularly evaluates customers and prospects based on a weighted list of criteria. The visualization of account value, using the formulas in this chapter, provides a tool that can help the many salespeople who still suffer with fear and anxiety. The incredibly dramatic growth of the building industry in the last half of the 1990s and the beginning of this decade has made the job of sales easier. The industry will eventually change. Sooner or later, a downturn in the economy will create challenges to your sales career. The abilities that you cultivate now will prepare you for those challenging times.

Dealer Strategies

Dealers employ the three methods of negotiation described earlier—combat, compromise or cooperate. Relationships between dealers and their suppliers are uniquely marked by the symbiosis that exists between the two entities. Dealers and their suppliers are seeking growth in market share and sales volume. To achieve that growth, they rely on each other

---

* The criterion related to this issue, while relevant on many levels to all architects, is primarily applicable to residential architects. Architects who design new homes and create remodeling plans are considered residential architects.

for sales, marketing, service, production, and delivery of materials. The relationship begins to twist and turn when the two entities begin to determine which party is responsible for the various contributions to the relationship.

Combative dealers adopt the strategy that they should hold their suppliers responsible for as much as possible. Their strategy is simply to *avoid commitments to suppliers and sell whatever customers ask for.* In other words, combative dealers prefer to develop situations in which they have access to as many product brands as possible. When customers ask for a specific brand, the dealer is happy to honor the request. Combative dealers sincerely believe it is the duty of the manufacturer to create brand-name awareness and sales opportunities. They further expect the manufacturer to provide after-sale service support, either through reimbursement for out-of-pocket expenses to the dealer, or through actual staffing of field service representatives. Dealers continually pressure manufacturers to sponsor events such as local trade shows, golf outings, promotional events, and the like. When the dealer's customers pressure for reduced pricing, the combative dealer is quick to shift the responsibility and pressure manufacturers to offer concessions on behalf of the dealer's customers. Dealer salespeople commonly leave the manufacturer out of the sales process and later expect the manufacturer to jeopardize their own profits based upon the (potentially deficient) sales skills of the dealer. Salespeople would be surprised to discover that their anxiety encourages combative relationships to develop. The salespeople expect combative negotiations and, not surprisingly, their expectations are fulfilled. The error many salespeople make, and their employers permit, is their failure to obtain commitments from dealers before they consummate the relationship.

Compromising dealers adopt the strategy to *cultivate relationships with manufacturers who provide good products, dependable service, and financial stability.* They recognize that they owe some degree of loyalty to suppliers. Although compromising dealers may not aggressively promote product brands, they are at least participants in the programs suppliers offer. Compromising dealers often limit the number of brands they support, with the expectation that their suppliers will offer similar loyalty. Compromising dealers are reasonable in their expectation of suppliers.

Cooperative dealers employ the strategy of aggressively striving to partner with suppliers to maximize market share. They seek relationships in which suppliers want to partner to outsell local competitors. These dealers market product brands aggressively by investing in showrooms, samples, sales support, service support, and more. In return, they expect suppliers, whether manufacturers or two-step distributors, to provide training, talented salespeople, quality products, and other forms of support. In some situations, the dealer and manufacturer jointly sponsor events and promotional programs. In nearly all situations, cooperative relationships between manufacturers and dealers are marked by mutual respect and cooperation, thus setting the relationship on a solid foundation.

The promotional role of the supplier's sales representative to the dealer is critically important. A highly skilled manufacturer representative can generate sales opportunities and dramatically enhance the relationship, while a poorly skilled manufacturer representative can quickly destroy the enthusiasm and trust of the dealer base.

Sales Strategies

In your promotional role, you will encounter three types of salespeople. They will display the same negotiating tactics as other adversaries—combative, compromising, or cooperative.

The strategy of the combative salesperson, and every salesperson for that matter, is *to make easy sales*. Why suffer when life can be easy! So dealer salespeople frequently invest their time farming with the customers with whom they have been doing business for many years. You well know that calling on established customers is much easier than prospecting for new accounts. Although the strategy (value) of salespeople is sales growth and a stated willingness to prospect aggressively, their tactics (behaviors) reflect differently. In your promotional roles, you will frequently discover that combative salespeople are resistant to your efforts. Many combative salespeople attempt to avoid work by passing it on to their promotional sales representative or coworkers. The strategies in this book will help you enroll the support of this reluctant audience.

A loftier sales strategy, found among compromising salespeople, is to *prospect aggressively for new sales opportunities*. Their stated value system—i.e., increase sales—is matched by their behavior. They are hard workers who strive to focus diligently on their daily tasks. These salespeople are eager consumers of your support and persistently follow up on sales opportunities. Compromising salespeople are eager to accept the help and promotional sales efforts from qualified sales mentors.

The most sophisticated salespeople are cooperative salespeople who *gain control of their career through the ongoing pursuit of skills and the development of loyal, profitable clientele*. These salespeople demonstrate an insatiable desire for growth, constantly studying the skills of the profession. These salespeople, even when they have achieved success, continue striving to build higher levels of skill and confidence in their careers. These are the rarest salespeople, and they often find themselves in mentoring roles.

Preparing for the Heat of Battle

At this point, you are prepared to create your own strategic game plan for battle. You should have surmised by now that a crucial strategy for success is the *selection of prospects with the most potential.* In addition to the factors discussed earlier—sales volume, long-term potential, and so on—you should be acutely aware that cooperative prospects and customers are profitable.

Cooperative prospects and customers are not necessarily the most profitable, however. You already know that many of the best customers in the industry are combative, by virtue of their success and power. The most successful builders, architects, and dealers are in positions that afford them negotiating clout. Rather than expect your customers and prospects to adapt to you, you should prepare yourself and be able to adapt to the various challenges and situations that will occur in the market.

CHAPTER FOUR

BUILDER
SALES STRATEGIES

It is easy to fall into the habit of bidding on projects and waiting for results to follow. A good term for this tactic is *bid and pray*. There is virtually no strategy involved. The tactic, as pointed out earlier, is a reaction to the pressures of the construction industry. This behavior wastes valuable time and creates only mediocre sales results.

Although bid and pray is the typical approach of many, if not most, salespeople in the building industry, they still manage to enjoy a satisfying career in which they make good money. They become satisfied with the money but still fail to achieve the sense of security and happiness that provides rewarding careers. For many, their core values tell them to find security through personal growth and pursuit of highly developed sales skills, while the successful accumulation of income sends conflicting signals. Thus, salespeople muddle along, continuing to bid on projects, satisfying themselves with average or mediocre results that allow them to "get by."

It is true enough that in some situations you have no choice but to bid and pray. If you feel forced into a bid-only situation, you may truly have to accept the parameters the customer sets forth, or you must choose not to bid at all. You must decide whether you are willing to offer a blind bid and hope that good results follow.

The difference between average salespeople and the true sales leaders of our industry is that the latter will explore the various options available before they decide on a course of action. Average salespeople make no attempt to consider alternative options to their methods. They see no options, and they feel they have no choices. The truth is that they have many choices.

> STRATEGY #1:
>
> Slow down the sales process
> and sweat the details.

The Good Strategy—Slow Down

One alternative to the common bid-and-pray tactic is to *slow down the sales process and sweat the details*. This strategy leads to:

- Better closing ratios
- Less wasted effort
- More credibility

You eventually have to offer a price before you can make the sale. Slowing down means that you take time in preparation with the customer *before* you submit a price. You will discover that the most immediate benefit is that chances for sales success increase. You can easily calculate the impact of this strategy. For example, if a slower, more deliberate process could increase your closing ratio from 10 percent to 20 percent, then you would be able to bid half as often to keep your business at the same level. Better yet, you would double your business if you doubled your closing ratio *and* kept the same level of sales activity.

Another benefit of this strategy is that you become much more efficient in your daily activities. As your closing ratio increases, you discover that you cannot cater to every whim of customers, and you need to become more selective in your activities. You discover that more choices become available to you as you increase your personal power. Most salespeople instantly say, "Whoa! This strategy may sound good on paper. But in the real world, I don't know . . ." In the real world, I have seen many salespeople test this strategy, and I have heard their testimonials that it works! More importantly, the builders with whom you work will actually begin to respect your attention to detail. Builders prefer to invest a few extra moments sweating the details to avoid costly mistakes.

Many construction-industry salespeople have not developed this strategic skill simply because their employers do not insist on it. As mentioned earlier, the training most salespeople receive focuses on product knowledge, not strategic selling. Thus, you may discover that you will need to independently develop your strategic sales abilities. But the idea of slowing down the process is nothing new. In fact, many organizations develop their entire sales model in a way that forces salespeople and customers to interact slowly before the salespeople deliver a price. This approach is common in the home-improvement industry: Some organizations insist that their salespeople conduct numerous meetings with clients before they deliver a price proposal.

The certainty you can count on is that, once you have given a price to a builder or remodeler, the sales process is instantly changed. Your value to customers is based initially on your ability to deliver prices and products. Customers will not ask you to become a credible expert upon which they can rely. You need to earn that rank. When you can defer the discussion on pricing, numerous benefits emerge, including a rise in your credibility. You naturally improve your chances for sales success as a result of the education you receive from your customers about their specific needs. When you slow down and customize proposals to the specific needs of your customers, you will discover that they are more interested in the potential of doing business with you and your company. The added benefit is that you save considerable time by avoiding errors and needlessly pricing projects for which you have little chance for success. When you slow down the process, you determine who is serious about doing business with you.

Case Studies

The trade-show "price question" response. Any salesperson who has ever worked at a trade show is familiar with the common question builders and remodelers pose. When builders are particularly interested in a product on display, they quickly ask salespeople, "How much does that cost?" Salespeople are so accustomed to receiving the question that they sincerely admit not knowing, but they gladly offer to contact the builder at a later date, when the builder and salesperson will have the opportunity to investigate mutual business interests and pricing options. When the builder persists by asking, "I'm just looking for a 'ball park' idea," salespeople smile and instinctively admit once again that they are in no position to provide a quick answer, justifying this position by reminding the builder that pricing would depend on many factors, such as volume, product specifications, special promotions, and the like.

In these situations, salespeople have no remorse about their unwillingness to instantly provide a price to builders, reasoning that they really do not know the pricing. They further recognize that builders are not in a position to purchase. Despite the fact that the builders receive no immediate price, the sales situation is not adversely affected.

The standard sales situation is really no different. The next time you feel pressured to quickly provide a price or lose a sales opportunity, remember that many salespeople have been in this situation before and have successfully deferred the discussion on pricing. Think about the trade show, and perhaps the image will help you find comfort in slowing the process.

A salesman says No. Bob, a Chicago salesman for a window distributor, had continually bid the windows for various builders in his marketplace. His common practice was to pick blueprints up at offices without the benefit of a physical meeting with the builder. Bob would submit prices and hope to meet with builders after they had reviewed his pricing. As you might expect, he sensed that he was getting a very low percentage of his bids. He had also discovered that numerous errors were costing his supplier money as a result of his haste. After Bob attended one of our training seminars, he decided to insist that builders permit a face-to-face meeting before he could offer a suitable window price. He reasoned with them that he needed the meeting to clarify details to save himself, and the builder, valuable time. At first, he was terrified to make this demand, and he was even more concerned when two builders told him that he could "bid the windows or take a hike." They essentially told him that he would play by their rules or not at all.

Bob decided to stick to his guns, concluding that he did not deserve that level of treatment and noting that those two builders had never purchased from him anyway. He also discovered many builders whom he had not met previously for any great length of time were suddenly meeting with him to discuss the details of their business. Bob concluded that he was saving himself huge amounts of time by not working with the uninterested builders. He maturely surmised that their lack of interest probably had little to do with him and more to do with their satisfaction with current suppliers. The biggest benefit for Bob in changing his approach was that he started selling more in less time. And he became happier.

Slowing Down the Sales Process

How do you slow down the sales process? Here are 10 tactics that will work:

1. Prospect more . . . and more. The easiest way to save yourself enormous amounts of time is to invest more time finding good prospects and customers. The rush to bid-and-pray tactics stems from the fear of angering a customer, and this fear arises from misperceptions about the abundance of market opportunities.

The number of prospects seems limited when you have not investigated all the potential gems of opportunity in the marketplace. This perception of limited prospects makes every prospect appear priceless. Your confidence soars when you believe that opportunities are plentiful. The only way to create the security of knowing that life provides abundant opportunities in sales is to prospect constantly. Develop an abundance of prospects to remind you that there are alternatives and choices in the marketplace.

---

10 TACTICS THAT SLOW DOWN THE SALES PROCESS

1. Prospect more . . . and more.
2. Make appointments to pick up blueprints.
3. Know the builder's business goals and history.
4. Qualify the builder's value to you.
5. Qualify the project specifications before you prepare a bid.
6. Get to know key people in the organization.
7. Pass on bids that you have little chance of winning.
8. Present the quote to decision-makers.
9. Don't believe everything builders tell you; they may be misinformed, not lying.
10. Know when and how to say "No."

---

2. Make appointments to pick up blueprints. This is a seemingly obvious tactic to employ. Despite the obvious, many salespeople arrive at jobsites and offices to obtain blueprints that have been left behind for them, and they don't meet the decision-maker before they prepare their price estimate. If customers do not believe you are worthy of a five-minute meeting to discuss a project, why would you invest hours preparing a price estimate?

3. Know the builder's business goals and history. If you have done your job well, then the builder will value you as more than an outsider, more than merely a person who sells materials. The builder will value you as a contributor (dare we say partner?) who provides benefit to the profitability of the organization. To achieve this status, you need to learn more about the builder. Many salespeople boast that they want to "partner" and "become a part" of the builder's organization. But frequently their sales behavior does not support this value. If salespeople are sincere in this value, then their behavior should match the value. They will take time to ask questions, and to understand the builder's marketing vision, operational challenges, sales challenges, and history.

4. **Qualify the builder's value to you.** Use appointments to learn as much as possible about the potential value the builder brings to you. You might discover that you would be foolish to invest the time required to service the builder according to his or her expectations. When a builder places unreasonable demands on you, you must decide at what price you need to conduct business to remain profitable for yourself and your employer. When you rush to bid on projects, your relationships feel project-driven and as short-term as a one-night stand. If you take the time to understand the builder's vision and the personal benefit for you, then you will enjoy business relationships based on long-term mutual benefit.

Consider developing a rating system similar to the one described in the first chapter. Rate all your customers and prospects based on the long-term *potential* they can provide to you as a supplier. A common mistake many salespeople make is to rate customers based on their purchasing history. The key to successful sales growth, however, is to evaluate your *future* opportunity, not your *past* results. Rate the future of your prospects and customers. Create simple categories (e.g., A = great customer/prospect; B = average customer/prospect; C = poor customer/prospect), and you will be amazed at the instinctive way you begin to improve your time management.

5. **Qualify the project specifications *before* you prepare a bid.** Once again, this might seem like an obvious tactic not worth mentioning. Yet salespeople and builders waste countless hours when projects are bid incorrectly or are bid with numerous "alternates." Nearly every product available in our industry today offers multiple options and features from which builders can choose. If you have done your research well (using the previous two tactics), you already are equipped to make product recommendations to builders. You must ask yourself, once again, whether a builder who is not willing to invest a few minutes of time to clarify details will value your time and skill.

6. **Get to know key people in the organization.** One sales fallacy that has existed for years is the old adage "You have to get to the decision-maker." The truth is that there is usually not *one* decision-maker in a given organization. In fact, many people influence decisions and product selection. A laborer who complains about the time wasted to install a product can change a company's decision regarding the future use of that product. A rude salesman can "turn off" a receptionist, who later is discovered to be the owner of the company. Great organizations value input from a variety of people. Great salespeople recognize this truth and strive to understand the dynamics of an organization before they rush to price products.

7. **Pass on bids that you have little chance of winning.** Sometimes, salespeople just know that they will not get the business, no matter how competitive their pricing. Yet they persist in offering pricing, making the assumption that it "can't hurt." In many of these situations, though, doing so *can* hurt. Some salespeople think that to at least give the builder a price is a sign of commitment and professionalism, and that doing so will impress the builder with their willingness to work hard. If an uncompetitive bid is offered, before the value of the product has been established, a builder may falsely assume you are overpriced, thus preventing future opportunities. The real problem is that everyone is wasting time needlessly when there is little chance to do business. Sales leaders maximize the value of time for everyone, admitting when it is better not to bid.

8. **Present the quote to decision-makers.** You just read that there is usually not one decision-maker, and so this tactic might seem rather hypocritical. The truth is that there are decision *influencers,* and you need to persuade someone that you are the star salesperson representing the best company in the field.

If you only fax a quote or "drop it off," you are leaving yourself vulnerable in numerous ways. The builder might misunderstand aspects of your bid. A competitor may present a bid in such a favorable light that your bid never receives proper scrutiny. The biggest concern you should have is that a builder (we are referring to a prospective customer who does not currently buy from you) will not have a great deal of respect for the time and effort you put into your work if you trivialize it by merely leaving it on a desk to be reviewed at someone's leisure. You work hard to price materials, and you should insist that your hard work is rewarded with at least a brief meeting to review the details.

> If an uncompetitive bid is offered, before the value of the product has been established, a builder may falsely assume you are overpriced, thus preventing future opportunities.

9. **Don't believe everything builders tell you; they may be misinformed, not lying.** Many salespeople make mistakes—we all know that. Builders also make blunders every now and then. Take time to verify details in the field. Get to know the real timeframes in which builders operate. The most common way in which to err as a salesperson is to accept statements that builders make about your competition. The builders are probably not lying to you, but they may be misinformed. Take time to get important details, and get them in writing if necessary.

10. **Know when and how to say No.** Sometimes, you have to say No. If you could provide customers with everything they wanted, when they wanted, and at the price they wanted, you would soon discover that your business suffers. You cannot be all things to all people. You should understand that many customers expect more than your company or you can offer.

There is no shame in admitting your limitations. But there is grave error in making promises that you can't keep. You must know when to say No.

The Great Strategy—Sell Profits, Not Price

A new opportunity will appear after you have learned to slow the sales process. You will become more aware of the point made in previous chapters, that your customers' ultimate concern is *profit, not price*. Builders obvi-

> STRATEGY #2:
>
> Sell profits, not price.

ously do not think twice about the difference in price between a power nail gun and a traditional hammer. The price of a nail gun is many times the price of a hammer, yet the price of the nail gun is meaningless to builders when they consider the dramatic reduction in labor costs it creates. It is easy to take the value of the nail gun for granted; it is easy to forget that a salesperson once had to persuade the builder to make a change and pay a much higher price for this more efficient tool.

Common sense suggests that the price of a nail gun is obviously worth the investment to builders. Your product probably offers similar features that, once discovered, will seem like common-sense sales opportunities. Unfortunately, common sense is not common practice. Many salespeople become so focused on price issues that they fail to recognize that the most important benefit they can provide is a way to improve their customers' profits. They hope and pray that price will be enough to earn them the sale.

Most salespeople behave in ways that suggest they can help reduce costs only with lower prices, but this is not the case. The builder's long-term cost and product profitability are affected by numerous factors other than price—e.g., installation costs, late deliveries, consumer brand awareness. So take time to consider every aspect of your product and service. When you have considered all the ways in which you can help your customers save money or increase their sales, then you should demonstrate these benefits to them.

Once again, if we recognize ourselves in this description, our values fail to match our behaviors. We understand that our job is to help our customers achieve higher profits, yet we react in a way that suggests cheap prices are the only method we have to help. We all must discover the "nail gun" advantage in our respective products and services. We must demonstrate ways in which our products and services enhance customers' profitability.

When you can develop tactics that demonstrate concern for your customers' profits, then numerous benefits will result. Customers will demonstrate their high opinion of you with loyalty and respect for your business ideas. Your employer and your peers will respect your business acumen. Most importantly, your self-confidence will grow exponentially.

The key to success in this strategy is *quantification*. There are three ways in which you can help builders increase their profits—lower costs, higher sales, and higher margins.

> There are three ways in which you can help builders increase their profits-lower costs, higher sales, and higher margins.

The previous strategy, slowing down the process, supports your ability to enhance customer profitability. If you are unable to slow the process to learn how your customers generate profits, you will not be able to help them. You need to discover the key issues involved in the builder's business model. You will strengthen relationships and increase your sales when you have a detailed understanding of the ways in which your customers generate profits. Your value to customers is more than the price of your products. Your value to customers is the "total cost" of doing business. If your product reduces installation costs, then that should be taken into account when calculating your value. If your product increases the profits to your customer, than this factor should be considered in your promotional efforts.

Take the time to calculate all the value that your product and service provides. The difference between the value of your product and the price is the total cost to your customer. While you are calculating the total value of your product and service, your competitors will still be talking about price and reacting to your proactive consultative approach.

> You are responsible for the quantification of value.

Your ability to demonstrate the profitability you provide your customers is contingent upon your ability to calculate those profits in very specific terms. Consider the following real-life examples:

Demonstrate increased profitability. A salesperson for a countertop manufacturer assured his customer that the product was so popular in the marketplace that it would reduce the customer's time to sell a home. The builder would easily recoup the costs of the upgrade plus the markup. The salesperson additionally estimated the savings in interest expense to the builder. After the salesperson estimated the value in interest savings, the builder volunteered that "even a two-week increase in turnover would justify the price on the countertop." If you're skeptical, consider that 6 percent interest on construction loans of $500,000 costs a builder $30,000 in annual interest. Two weeks of savings is nearly $1,200! Another motivating factor for builders is their competition. Builders will be fearful that a competitor will be the first to realize this savings and competitive edge.

Calculate cost savings. During one of our sales-training seminars, a salesperson complained that his competitor was $.50 cheaper per square of shingle roofing. Fifty cents. He was extremely agitated with his employer for not matching the price. The salesperson additionally volunteered that prospects were complaining that the same competitor was frequently late on deliveries, sometimes promising morning deliveries and not arriving until the afternoon. Seminar attendees also learned that a different competitor, with prices also $.50 lower per square, did not have a boom truck to load the shingles on the roof of the home. This salesperson was allowing the lower prices of his competitors to unnecessarily create agitation and fear.

It didn't take a rocket scientist to figure out the benefit his company *could* provide to customers. In fact, a three-hour delay in delivery might justify a difference of *$5 per square* of roofing material. A typical roof takes about 20 squares of roofing material. The savings of $.50 per square equals approximately $10 per roof. Quantifying the total cost savings to the customer in this situation would seem an easy task.

If a crew of three roofers—at a total labor and overhead cost of approximately $50 per hour—is forced to wait an entire morning to receive delivery of materials, then a delay of three hours in delivery creates an additional $150 in labor costs for the contractor. In this example, the *price* savings of $10 per roof was adding $150 to the labor *cost* of the late delivery! The cost savings of a rooftop delivery can be calculated in a similar way by simply multiplying labor rates by the time it takes laborers to carry materials up to the roof.

Provide a competitive edge with a unique product feature. A few suppliers of windows offer unique features that allow builders to distinguish their products. The average salesperson describes these unique features and *waits for the builders to figure out* how the features may be of benefit.

In one situation, a popular window brand offers a unique feature of Venetian blinds between the panes of glass in the window. The person who sells this feature reminds the builder of the savings this creates for the builder's customers, savings of the additional cost of window treatments. This unique feature is both extremely popular with homeowners and exclusive to this window manufacturer, which creates a competitive edge that easily defeats other window salespeople.

Another example involves a manufacturer who produces unique wood species on the interior of the window. A builder is quick to ask about the costs. When a salesperson responds that an upgrade of oak or mahogany increases the price by 30 percent, the builder balks instantly. However, there is a better way to demonstrate the competitive edge.

The proper way to highlight the benefit of this option would be to remind builders that the product feature might help them distinguish the entire home. For example, builders might want to highlight a signature room in a house. Perhaps an oak window over the kitchen sink would be a unique way to match the oak cabinetry. Or two mahogany windows that match the paneling in a home office would set these builders' entire houses apart from other builders with whom they compete. "The key," the salesperson would explain, "is that you can use the wonderful feature on just a few windows to highlight those signature rooms, *without destroying the overall window budget*." The salesperson who takes this approach slows the process while establishing value. At the same time, builders are free to ponder a unique method for distinguishing their homes for increased profits by way of quicker turnover or an increased price for the house . . . or both!

Provide a competitive edge by introducing a new product or service. Imagine a situation in which a sale of only two hundred dollars might help you solidify a relationship worth tens of thousands of dollars per year. One manufacturer has trained dealer salespeople throughout the country to introduce a product as a way for remodelers to accomplish this amazing strategy.

Home-improvement contractors routinely sell the advantages of vinyl siding or windows in hopes of distinguishing their services from competitors. Unfortunately for these contractors, the story always sounds the same. Some remodelers are learning to distinguish their sales effort from others by introducing homeowners to decorative polyurethane millwork options, such as window crossheads and exterior door trim, in addition to vinyl siding or replacement windows. The low-maintenance product fits in beautifully with the low-maintenance siding, while providing the traditional look of wood that distinguishes the home.

The return on the investment for contractors is significant as a result of the improved margins they receive on the incremental sale of the decorative options. A sale of just $300 supports a much larger sale of $8,000. Remodelers' customers are thrilled by the surprising improvement to the appearance of their homes. The result for contractors is satisfied customers who provide more income and referrals. The secret to success for these remodelers begins with a salesperson.

The manufacturer of millwork who recognized this opportunity is providing a strong example with a training program that demonstrates how to create opportunities at all levels of the building industry. The training program is helping the organization's salespeople, its dealers'

10 WAYS YOU CAN ENHANCE YOUR CUSTOMER'S PROFITS

1. Quantify the value of product features.
2. Present the profit value of *you*.
3. Train builders' salespeople on the unique product features that benefit the consumer.
4. Train the installation team.
5. Provide ideas on ways for builders to gain a competitive edge.
6. Quantify the before-sale service value of your company.
7. Quantify the after-sale service value of your company.
8. Demonstrate how your company's profitability is important to your costumers.
9. Compare your product enhancements to alternatives.
10. Know when to say "Not now."

salespeople, and the remodelers' salespeople. It is a formula that can work for you.

Enhancing Customer Profits

Here are 10 ways you can enhance your customers' profits:

1. **Quantify the profit value of product features.** Feature-benefit presentations frequently address exactly the product features that should be of interest to builders or remodelers while they fail to identify the correct product value.

For example, salespeople in the window industry persist in describing the energy efficiency of windows, specifically noting the special low-emissivity, commonly known as "Low-E," coating on the surface of the glass. The coating is an oxidized metal, which hardly changes the appearance of the glass while it improves energy efficiency. The problem is that many consumers remain unaware of the technology. Therefore, builders are being asked to incur an expense that their customer, the consumer, does not value.

There is a better way for salespeople to sell the benefit of the thermal-glass technology. Rather than lecture builders on the wonderful benefits of the glass, they should focus on presenting supplemental literature and sales aids that builders can use in promoting their homes. For example, they might recommend a training seminar for builders' salespeople. Another approach might focus on a point-of-purchase display in model homes that educates the builders' customers about the benefits of high-performance glass.

The best sales approach is *not* focused on presenting to someone with no stake in the product benefit, the builders. The builders are not living in the homes and paying the heating bills. The best approach focuses on helping builders sell the benefits to the audience most affected by the technology, the consumers. Salespeople could remind builders that when the consumers recognize the quality of that single component of the home they will appropriately realize that the builders probably put that same level of quality into every component. The benefits include faster sales, more satisfied customers, and higher prices for their homes.

2. **Present the profit value of you.** When was the last time you shared a solid sales lead with a builder or remodeler? I've met salespeople who have never provided even one sales lead to a builder during their career. Consider how many times you have been frustrated because your customers asked you for a 1 percent price reduction. Try to recall the fear you have frequently experienced as you debated how to handle this challenging situation.

The best example I have ever been able to provide salespeople occurred on a weekday morning when I walked into my bank to protest a $60 fee. My banker invited me into his office to discuss the situation. He calmly accepted my threat to take all of my business (business checking, personal checking, and investment management accounts) to another financial services firm. He explained that I needed to fill out a simple piece of paper to avoid a charge like that again, and he asked me a few pointed questions about my business.

I was still angry, but I was happy to discuss my business with anyone who would listen. If you observe carefully, you will discover that most people's favorite subject of conversation is themselves. I was no different. So I happily explained the business model of my sales-training company. My banker ended our discussion by saying, "See? *This* is what we need to be talking about! I know people who need sales training and would benefit from a guy like you." I did not get my $60 back, but I can easily say that I walked out of his office with a sense of pride, and I hoped that he might actually refer a client to me.

One week later, I saw my banker again, and he introduced me to a company that specializes in air-filtration systems. I ended up conducting a one-day seminar for that company, for which I charged my normal daily fee (significantly higher than the $60). After an experience like that with your banker, how much would you worry about the additional $60 price for services? You probably would become a loyal customer to a salesperson like that, which is exactly what I did. You have every opportunity to build the same loyalty in your customers by providing leads, sales ideas, networking opportunities, technical assistance, and more.

3. **Train builders' salespeople on the unique product features that benefit the consumer.** There are literally thousands of ways in which salespeople can take advantage of this opportunity. The majority of innovations over the past few decades have been designed to reduce maintenance and improve the quality of homes—synthetic decking, cement fiber siding, vinyl products, recycled materials, propelene house wraps, and engineered lumber, to name only a few. Salespeople should constantly point out more to builders than how these features benefit homeowners. Salespeople should take time to educate builders, using available tools such as videos, literature, press clippings, and the like, on the ways *they can educate their customers*.

4. **Train the installation team.** Nothing impresses builders more than salespeople who can roll up their sleeves and work with the products they sell. That much is obvious. If you can physically demonstrate how to work with your products, you obviously will earn your customers' respect. Unfortunately, not all salespeople are as mechanically skilled as the industry professionals to whom they sell (I am all thumbs and two left feet, so I can personally vouch for that!). In lieu of physically demonstrating how to work with a product, a sales leader may find alternative ways to create necessary training, using available tools such as videos, installation instructions, or possibly even inviting a respected industry expert to conduct a seminar. Another way a salesperson might help with installation challenges would be

to introduce builders to each other so they can exchange ideas regarding their construction methods. Whatever methods you choose, always remember to calculate the labor time you have saved the builder.

5. **Provide ideas on ways for builders to gain a competitive edge.** Subtle trends are continually evolving while builders and remodelers are caught up in the challenges of their day-to-day activity. One salesman I worked with casually mentioned to a builder that he noticed a lot of houses were being built with laundry rooms on the second floor, which saved the inhabitants the trouble of carrying loads of laundry up and down flights of stairs. I was surprised (although I should not have been) that the builder was unaware of this evolving trend in the market. The salesperson suggested that the builder walk through the models and offered to introduce the builder to a few of the progressive builders in the market. The builder was grateful for the idea and took the salesperson's advice, along with the introductions. This seems like an obvious practice, yes? I found out that quite a few builders respected similar advice from this Toledo sales representative.

6. **Quantify the before-sale service of your company.** The roofing sales example noted earlier provides an excellent example of how you can quantify timely delivery to save builders money.

7. **Quantify the after-sale service value of your company.** The after-sale service of a window dealer is critical to a builder's success. Many window dealers rely on the service the manufacturer supplies, but most builders will tell you they prefer to work with a dealer who provides local service, as well. In the window business, the question is not *if* something will go wrong; the question is *when*. If you have a local service representative, you might be able to save the builder thousands of dollars per year between reduced customer call-backs and good will.

One remodeler near Fort Wayne, Indiana loves to boast of the exceptional service he receives from the local salesperson of heating and ventilation equipment. When the remodeler had problems servicing a heating unit, he was astonished when the salesperson, a woman, was able to tell him the year and model of the machine and even some installation idiosyncrasies of which the builder should be aware. The remodeler says, "You can't put a value on that type of service." Actually you can . . . and you should! That remodeler probably pays himself $2,000 per week. For every hour of time the salesperson saves him, she gives that builder $80 (assuming that the remodeler is working a 50-hour week).

Hopefully, you are beginning to believe that you can quantify anything.

8. **Demonstrate how your company's profitability is important to your customers.** Many builders "require" suppliers to make separate deliveries of windows and the corresponding window screens. Worth noting in an example like this is that two issues are relevant. First, the salesperson should attempt to verify whether this is a common practice that all competitors in the marketplace offer. Second, whether or not the practice is com-

mon, and even if the builder will not pay extra for the service, the sales-person should strive to impress upon the builder what additional costs a dealer incurs for extra deliveries. Many salespeople will state, "Builders do not care. They merely feel it is up to the supplier to manage the profitability of their business." Salespeople need to question whether those are the builders they want to do business with. If nothing else, they need to respect that all services come with a cost that someone must pay. If a supplier is not profitable, then that supplier will eventually cut back on services, and the builder-supplier relationship will suffer. Salespeople are permitted to request a fair margin on their prices. Ideally, they want to find as many customers as possible who offer a heartfelt desire of mutual benefit.

9. **Compare your product enhancements to alternatives.** As an example of this tactic, engineered lumber products have emerged as standard items in the construction industry. These products were not readily accepted only a few short years ago. The emergence of these products has resulted from the cost benefits they provide in the form of lower prices.

10. **Know when to say "Not now".** Salespeople frequently assume that No means No. Sometimes, however, No is not No but is instead Not now. Just because your price is too high this time does not mean you should auto-matically strive to get the sale at any price. Sometimes, your competitors are pricing too low, at a level they can not support profitably for the long term. Do not assume that a negative answer is the end of the sales process; it may merely signify that the timing is not right for this sale. If you hold your price and lose a sale (now), you may later discover that the customer comes back to you with a solid expectation that he or she will be paying more and get-ting more in return.

Final Word

Salespeople commonly make the mistake of assuming that presentations should consist of boasts and dramatic claims of service performance (i.e., feature-benefit presentations). They fail to realize that these types of pre-sentations are cliché. The real key to presentation success is to stick to impressive facts, not opinions. Your ability to *quantify the value* of your products and services will give you credibility that your competitors cannot match. Your customers will gain more respect for you, and, more impor-tantly, you will feel more self-respect as a result of your business-like approach to conducting business.

CHAPTER FIVE

ARCHITECT
SALES STRATEGIES

To many industry professionals, the role of the architect remains mysterious. Many people judge their role as superfluous, a necessary evil created by industry regulators and local building inspectors. This perception is unfortunate because architects provide valuable services that help standardize industry practices and contractual arrangements. The architectural profession provides design concepts and legal documents to regulate construction practices.

The two trade associations that regulate the majority of architectural practices are the Construction Specifications Institute (CSI) and the American Institute of Architects (AIA). The CSI is an organization devoted to standardizing methods of construction documentation and industry definitions. The AIA regulates the education of architects and is heavily involved in the design of contracts that are used to regulate relationships between builders and owners. considering a membership in your local chapters of both organizations is worthwhile, to investigate ways in which you might become more involved, much in the same way as associate members contribute their efforts to the National Association of Home Builders (NAHB).

Stages of the Construction Process

Among the various practices and definitions that architects influence are the terms related to the stages in the construction process. The CSI has defined the stages of the construction process as follows:

- **Planning**—The feasibility and preliminary budgeting of a project. Issues related to zoning, use of the structure, and return on investment are considered at this time.
- **Design**—The style and function of the project. The design phase is broken down into three stages (noted below).
- **Bid**—During this stage, contractors, subcontractors, and suppliers provide cost estimates for materials and labor to complete the project.
- **Construction**—The project construction phase where the structure is built.
- **Post-construction**—Often overlooked by salespeople, the time during with a structure is in use, maintained, and renovation projects are considered.

The CSI estimates that up to 70 percent of time invested in construction occurs in the *design* phase. The design phases are further subdivided into the following subcategories, whose terminology you should know:

- **Schematic design**—During schematic design, the owner and the architect determine the style and function of a project. They determine the project's budget constraints and physical limitations.
- **Design development**—During the design development phase, specific details of the project are determined and product choices are discussed.
- **Construction documents**—In the construction document stage, the final drawings, specifications, and other related documents are prepared for the next stage, the bid.

In spite of the many relevant decisions made during the design phase of construction, the majority of salespeople do not involve themselves until the bid stage. But by that time it is often too late to influence product selection. Thus, salespeople who are involved with architects and designers early in the process stand a better chance of involving themselves in the selection of products.

Architects are often involved during the bid and construction stages of the project. Some contractual arrangements between owners and architects require the architects to supervise construction details. At the very least, the architects are in a position to review the builders' work to ensure that it satisfies the contractual arrangements detailed in the construction documents.

The ABCs of Selling Architects

The first key to architectural sales success begins with the proper selection of your target architectural accounts. Numerous factors will influence the types of architects you should pursue. For example, a salesperson who attended one of my seminars worked in a very rural area in the upper peninsula of Michigan. There were probably only 10 architects in his market, and it didn't matter to him whether they worked for the owner of the project, or for the builder or the mayor. The size of his tight-knit community dictated that he would need to have a strong relationship with all industry professionals.

Alternatively, salespeople working in San Francisco would discover that there are thousands of architectural firms with whom they could work. The San Francisco sales representative would need to carefully select architects based on the influence they wield in the product-selection process.

The type of products you sell will also dictate the architects you pursue. A salesperson who markets high-performance glass walls would be more successful with a large architectural/engineering firm that designs high-rise buildings. A sales representative who sells decorative fabrics for commercial office space will have the most success with an architect specializing in interior design. A salesperson who sells decorative counter tops for residential construction will discover that bigger is not always better, eventually learning that relatively small firms, the designers of custom homes, are the best architects to approach. You will also discover by trial and error which architects provide the best sales opportunities. Once you have discovered which type of architects work best for your products, you should seek out those firms.

The size of the firm is unimportant; you need to have relationships with only a few good architects in your market. The stumbling block for many salespeople is that they try to foster relationships with too many architects. When it comes to architectural sales relationships, even a few architects can generate a large volume of business. Quality is better than quantity. You will need to dedicate significant effort to those architects with whom you build relationships. Numerous sales calls and administrative tasks will often be necessary to cultivate strong relationships. Thus, you should be selective about the architects with whom you work.

You should not view architects as a "special" audience that is to be treated separately. You should make architectural sales calls a part of your weekly activity. Your success with architects will result from a steady discipline of sales behavior that is similar, if not identical, to the tactics you use with builders. You will conclude that architects are potential jewels who you can simply evaluate using the same methods you use to rate other sales opportunities: A = extremely valuable prospects; B = very valuable prospects; C = poor prospects.

Salespeople who enthusiastically decide to sell to architects, however, often run out of gas before they achieve the desired success. They become excited about the potential opportunity architects provide, and then they go overboard in their efforts. They focus too much energy on architectural sales and are disappointed when they do not achieve immediate results. So you will need to strike a balance between the daily challenges of quoting, ordering, service, and prospecting with builders and with architects.

The most successful sales representatives keep a list of architects in their single database of prospects and customers. Then, when they are in a particular geographic location within their territory, they can efficiently include brief visits to architects to improve their time management. For example, if you were to discover that an architect offered the potential of $100,000 in annual business referrals, you might rate that architect as an A. Adding this jewel to your target list is precisely how you convert your vision of your territory from the sparse view depicted in Chapter 3, Figure 3.3, to the abundant view depicted in Figure 3.4.

The pharmaceutical industry focuses significant promotional effort on creating a sales structure that never works directly with the paying customer, the patient, or even the direct supplier of materials, the pharmacist. Pharmaceutical sales representatives regularly promote their products to doctors. To do so is logical because doctors are the authors of medical prescriptions, which are later fulfilled by the pharmacists who supply medicine to the doctors' patients. The sales representatives never meet the purchaser of materials. Similarly, in many situations, the architect who writes construction specifications is as influential as the doctor who writes medical prescriptions and therefore should receive more of the salesperson's focus and time.

To promote actively to children, toys, playgrounds, and "happy meals" have become part of the advertising landscape for fast-food restaurants. Although the children are not the purchasers of meals, their influence in the decision-making process is strong. Likewise, architects frequently influence the product-selection process of the ultimate purchasers of materials—the builders and homeowners.

Sales Strategies to the Architect

According to a study conducted by Hanley-Wood, a leading publisher of industry periodicals, architects ranked their preferred methods for receiving product information. Architects stated that these resources, in order of importance, are:

1. Product catalogs
2. Local product representatives
3. Trade/professional magazine editorials
4. Manufacturers' salespeople
5. Magazine advertising
6. Display showrooms
7. Consumer magazine editorials

This list hopefully ends the ongoing debate between dealer salespeople and manufacturer representatives regarding whose responsibility it is to be the sales representative for architects. It should come as no surprise to anyone in the industry that architects prefer, as the list notes, that local sales representatives become their primary contact point for product information. This makes sense because architects want quick access to specifications, literature, pricing, samples, data, and other information that is readily available from their local sales representatives. Architects would be remiss in their duties if they were to select products that were difficult to obtain and that were lacking in local representation.

Dealer sales representatives state that manufacturer representatives are responsible for "getting products specified" with architects, reasoning that these representatives benefit from the specification. The dealer sales representatives seem to conveniently forget that they will enjoy the benefit of the transaction, as well. It is vitally important that a salesperson fully recognize that, whether the architect's clients are the owners or the builders, no sale is complete until the purchase order is signed and all parties—owners, architects, and contractors—are satisfied. Thus, a *specification* is a recommended selection of a product, not the sale itself. The sale is the *transaction*. Dealer sales representatives who are waiting for manufacturer sales representatives to "get products speced" are tacitly giving control and power of their marketplace to the manufacturer sales representatives.

Dealer sales representatives who are willing to invest a small percentage of their time working with architects will discover that their efforts result in more transactions with builders. The sale is not theoretical to the architect; a transaction must eventually occur. These realities favor those salespeople who can establish a strong relationship with *all* the industry professionals involved in both the design and construction of the project. The architect and builder do not buy only products; they buy *you!*

You probably agree that very few salespeople would treat a potential builder with the disrespect of saying, "Hey there. I'll ignore you until you have a project that I can bid on, then I'll give you some attention. If I don't get that project, then I will ignore you until the next opportunity." That would be ridiculous. To sell one project to a builder, you might call on that builder for a period of months, or even years. You would keep the builder informed of industry events and product innovations. You would regularly visit with the builder to develop and strengthen a solid business relationship. You would certainly recognize that a strong business relationship is a result of persistence, loyalty, and dependability.

A relationship with an architect is no different. If you believe that there is opportunity within the architectural community, then you should agree that business relationships with architects are forged in the same way as those with builders. While your competitors are busy ignoring architects, an outstanding opportunity awaits if you take the time to evaluate those diamonds in the rough. To the accomplished industry professional, the ABCs of selling architects look very similar to the ABCs of selling builders. In the end, the only satisfactory approach to selling architects is to *treat them as paying customers.*

The Good Strategy—Treat Them as Paying Customers . . . and Get Paid!

> STRATEGY #3:
>
> Treat architects as paying customers—because they are!

In this section, consider the tactics carefully. You will discover situations in which salespeople fail to treat their *actual* paying customers as paying customers. During a sales-management meeting, the vice president of sales for a manufacturer noted that the relationship with an $80-million customer had deteriorated. The regional sales manager, because of his lack of contact with this valuable customer, was confronted by the vice president. The manager became defensive and responded, "I have sent them e-mails and letters. My phone number is on the bottom of my card and on my written communications. They are free to call me, but I haven't heard from them." He simply did not understand how his actions might have contributed to the decline of the relationship. He was waiting for the customer to call him! It is obviously the salesperson's responsibility to cultivate the relationship, not the customer's. Consider how these tactics apply to your interactions with all types of paying customers.

Architects deserve to be treated as paying customers. The tactics of this section will provide ideas about how you can foster stronger relationships with architects, not to mention builders, remodelers, and dealers. Keep in mind that architects do provide actual revenue. They might not spend a dime in your showroom, but the referrals and recommendations they make to their clients frequently provide more profit and revenue than a one-time check. Treat architects as paying customers—because they are!

---

10 TACTICS THAT TREAT THEM AS PAYING CUSTOMERS

1. Plan to build a relationship.
2. Evaluate account potential.
3. Make repeated sales calls.
4. Track your activity and opportunities with each firm.
5. Get to know everyone at the firm.
6. Offer training events (e.g., box lunches).
7. Don't wait until the bid phase to get involved in the sales process.
8. Provide support to help them service their clients.
9. Respect their time.
10. Know when to "walk."

Treating Them As Paying Customers

To treat architects and other clients as paying customers, adopt the following 10 tactics:

1. **Plan to build a relationship.** This tactic is essentially a repetition of the strategy itself, or so it would seem. There is, however, genuine benefit to stating to oneself, "I am going to strive to build relationships with a few quality architects in my market. I will attempt to make at least a few architectural sales calls every week. I may not develop relationships with very many. In fact, I might have only three or four architects with whom I work. But those few architects will be a great source of growth for me, and I will be a valuable resource for them." If you can commit yourself to this statement, then you have already won the battle.

And remember that it is going to be difficult at first. You may struggle to develop your architectural sales skills. But the difficulty of the struggle makes the effort worth it. Remember that most salespeople will give up quickly. Your persistence will pay dividends in the long run and distinguish you from your competitors.

2. **Evaluate account potential.** You would not persistently call on a builder or remodeler who had potential to purchase only a few hundred dollars of material from you annually. Not all builders are created equal. The same is true of architects, and perhaps more so. Review some of the information from Chapter 2 to help you determine your target audience. Rate each individual architect you meet. When you feel you have discovered a dozen who offer real potential, keep working with them. You won't win them all, but eventually a few of them will become loyal customers. Employ a standard system that lets you rate all categories of customer—i.e., builders, remodelers, architects, and dealers—on a similar scale. For example, if you choose to rate builders using rating symbols of A, B, and C, then use the same method for all accounts.

3. **Make repeated sales calls.** Can you imagine a salesperson achieving any dramatic success with a builder or dealer or remodeler by making a call only when there was a potential sale? Of course not. Great salespeople are in frequent contact with customers and prospects because they recognize the importance of being "in the know." Keep in frequent contact with architects by offering valuable information and intelligent questions every time you meet them.

You probably have various samples, literature, and technical information that you can provide. A common error salespeople make—with architects, builders, and dealers—is that they try to deliver *all* the information they can on *every* sales call. You have an abundance of information, and you need to recognize how unlikely it is that any customer will absorb everything during a brief introductory presentation. Instead of trying to saturate your customers and prospects with lots of data they will quickly forget, give them a sprinkling of information every time you visit. Repetition is the mother of learning.

Repetition is the mother of learning.

A first sales call to an architect may require only the delivery of a basic product catalog to supplement your meeting. If you discover potential for a relationship, you can bring more detailed information on a subsequent visit. As the relationship develops, you can offer additional literature, samples, information on CD, and more. If you attempt to give a customer all the information you have on an initial visit, you may be wasting valuable resources needlessly. More importantly, you will eliminate reasons for future visits. Build your relationship by offering educational information at regular intervals.

4. **Track your activity and opportunities with each firm.** Salespeople are notorious for their lack of administrative skills. It is not unusual to observe a salesperson who discovers opportunities worth thousands of dollars yet fails to write down the details regarding the opportunity. Computer

spreadsheets and databases provide ideal methods to monitor the opportunities. Monitoring opportunities with architects is especially important. You will discover many sales opportunities while architects are in the design phase of the process; bid opportunities may take months to materialize. During the development of a project—during the schematic design and design development stages—you may have numerous opportunities to assist. If you have no method for documenting and tracking the opportunities, the valuable chances will soon fall by the wayside.

5. **Get to know everyone at the firm.** A common error salespeople make, probably because of their project-driven focus with architects, is to concentrate all their sales efforts on only one person at a firm. The architectural profession is unique in that individual architects are transient and very upwardly mobile. An assistant architect at one firm often is the partner in his or her own firm within a few short years. You never know what wonderful opportunities may emerge tomorrow from a casual relationship you cultivate today.

6. **Offer training events (e.g., box lunches).** Read this suggestion carefully. Provide training events when appropriate but *do not assume that the objective of your relationship with an architect is to offer a box lunch.* (A *box lunch* is a scheduled presentation during which the staff of an architectural firm listens to a product presentation while they eat lunch provided by the presenters. A box lunch is a convenient method for getting information into the hands of a large audience.) During my career, I have made more than 7,000 architectural sales calls, and I can assure any salesperson that a box lunch is not the manna from heaven that provides instant income and rewards. In fact, a box lunch offered prematurely can potentially destroy momentum in a burgeoning relationship. The success of your box lunch, like many aspects of a sales relationship, hinges on the timing of the event. The box lunch should occur after you have made a few calls on the architectural firm. You should establish rapport with at least one or two architects within the practice and have a good understanding of the firm's scope of work before you schedule such a lunch.

7. **Don't wait until the bid phase to get involved in the sales process.** Start your involvement during the design phase. Your first introduction to an architect often results from an opportunity presented to you during the bid stage. Most salespeople reactively sell to architects, striving to change existing product specifications. You will discover that architects resist changes, and rightly so. If you approach architects with the hope of persuading them to change their specification, you may be successful, but do not be disappointed if you fail. Even if you fail in your effort to change the specification, you should still recognize that there might be numerous other projects in the design phase. Recognizing that your objective should be to get the next project is more important. These are the projects for which the architect will have an open mind and a willing ear.

8. **Provide support to help architects service their clients.** Just like builders, dealers, remodelers, and even you, architects need literature, sam-

ples, and technical information for communication with their clients. Try to understand the methods by which they sell to their clientele, and then offer the tools (e.g., samples, literature, spec sheets) that can help them in their effort.

9. **Respect their time.** This fact was mentioned earlier but bears repeating: Architects are paid for their time. Your ability to efficiently communicate information in a timely way will enhance your credibility. While we are on the subject, think about managing your time with all your customers and prospects more effectively. For salespeople to loiter during sales meetings in the hope that a mystical event will create a sale is a common emotional response. Exceed expectations by finishing meetings before prospects and customers expect you to. If you leave them wanting more, you will be a welcome visitor in the future. If you overextend your welcome, you may not get a second chance.

10. **Know when to "walk."** Sometimes, there is no relationship to cultivate. There are times when an architect (or any prospect) is simply not interested in you, your company, or your products. Don't fight the forces of the universe. Move on. Get the next one.

The Great Strategy—Establish Credibility

> STRATEGY #4:
>
> Position yourself as an expert
> to establish credibility.

Ben Franklin said, "A slip of the foot you will soon get over. A slip of the tongue you may never recover." This is how credibility works. History is full of stories about businessmen, politicians, actors, and other celebrities who were in the midst of successful careers when one event soured their entire image. The lesson we can learn from these people is that our credibility is precious. How you protect your personal image is the heart and soul of your career.

Credibility is like a balloon. You start out with a deflated balloon that is airless and limp, nothing more than potential to be inflated. As you blow up the balloon, it takes on shape, color, and beauty. It doesn't take much to destroy the balloon. One prick from a stickpin will destroy it beyond repair. Credibility can be deflated just as quickly.

Two components make up credibility—trust and knowledge. To merely have knowledge of your product isn't enough. Your customers also must believe they can trust your opinion as that of an objective expert. Credibility does not result from the title on your business card. Credibility is larger than that. You can establish credibility and credentials only by your repeated demonstration of knowledge and dependability.

When it comes time to sell to architects, credibility is the key to your success. The modern architectural profession is based on the avoidance of liability. Architects create legal documents that are subject to a variety of building-code regulations. An architect constantly battles the delicate challenge of creating aesthetically pleasing design that provides function while fulfilling clients' functional needs. The architect is faced with thousands of individual choices on any given project. These choices are magnified by an environment plagued with the constant evolution of product choices, technology, and regulatory challenges. It is little wonder that the architect wants and desires the highest level of expertise in a sales advisor.

Case Studies

The Tile Lady. In Chicago, Illinois a woman sold tiles for a local distributor of fancy decorative tiles. She regularly called on architects to promote her products and supplied them with samples. There was nothing special about her doing that. What was special about her was that she frequently helped architects and builders locate products that she did *not* sell. In other words, she actually referred customers to her competition! Imagine how trustworthy she must have appeared in the eyes of these architects. If you assume that she became a primary resource of information whenever these people had a question about tiles, you are correct. She became known to many of her customers simply as The Tile Lady. They had confidence that, no matter what their needs, they could rely on her for a trustworthy answer. That she sold a lot of tile for her own company probably doesn't need to be mentioned. As a result of her credibility, she was always the first person her customers called when they had a project, and she was the only person they needed to speak with to gain an honest answer.

The Two-Call Closer. A Kansas City salesman is in the home improvement sales business. He defies the tradition of this business by intentionally avoiding high-pressure sales tactics that are designed to make homeowners purchase on the first sales call. In an industry in which salespeople regularly strive for the one-call close, he has developed tactics to actually plan a two-call close. He figures that closing 50 percent of the time based upon a two-call process is better than closing only 15 percent of the time based on one-call closing tactics. His methods are simple. He merely educates his customers on the first call, but not necessarily in the ways you would expect. In addition to teaching them all the features and benefits of the product, he also gives them a brief education in purchasing tactics and ways to slow down high-pressure salespeople. The salespeople who call on his customers after his first call are probably very frustrated when they meet homeowners who are well-educated in the tactics of purchasing and negotiation. This is also an example of a salesperson using a strategy from the previous chapter—Slow Down and Sweat the Details—as well as the useful strategy from this chapter. He establishes credibility by providing an education way beyond product features and benefits. He establishes himself in the credible role of consultant to his homeowner customers.

Violation of the Rule. I will never forget the day I called on an architect who taught me the importance of sticking to my word. The architect was actually recommending my product to his customers, in spite of the fact that he wasn't thrilled with the level of service I had been providing. I had met with him once, and I attempted to meet again later on several occasions, to share new information on my company's products. One day, I called and asked for an appointment. He cautiously asked me whether I was really going to share new information about updated product features, or whether this was merely a sales call. I assured him that we had product innovations that he might want to know about, which was true. I asked for only 5 minutes of his time. He tersely responded that I had "said it would take *only 5 minutes* the last time I was in, and it ended up being close to 15!" Naturally, I was embarrassed by my behavior. I instantly thought to myself that 15 minutes shouldn't be so much to ask for. Then I quickly dismissed this thought, realizing that this architect would be out of business if he spent 15 minutes a week with all the potential vendors with whom he could do business. As you might expect, I assured him that I would use 5 minutes or less, and, if I didn't, he should kick me out of his office. The meeting lasted 4 minutes, and I was on my way to inflating the credibility balloon once again.

10 WAYS YOU CAN ESTABLISH CREDIBILITY

1. Never denigrate your competitors.
2. Compliment your competitors.
3. Stick to the agreed timeframe of your sales call.
4. Do what you said you would do.
5. Educate your customers about your products in a general way.
6. Present the innovations of your company.
7. Volunteer the limitations of your own product and service.
8. Send thank-you notes.
9. Drink water and eat mints.
10. Take notes!

Establishing Credibility

To establish credibility with our customers, both architects and others, develop your skills with the following 10 tactics:

1. **Never denigrate your competitors.** It is common for salespeople to share their opinions of their competition with architects. They will typically criticize their competitors or draw comparisons. They draw comparisons with the intention of placing their products in a favorable light. They mislead themselves into believing that, by drawing comparisons, they are not denigrating their competitors. But this run-of-the-mill tactic frequently fails.

When salespeople use this tactic, they forget that the architects have probably met the competitors' sales representatives. They believe that, by drawing comparisons, they have cleverly invented a unique method to discredit the competition. However, the opposite reaction usually occurs. They actually discredit themselves! Would you expect architects to accept the opinions of competing salespeople about *your* product? Of course not. So why would you expect to gain credibility by offering negative opinions about your competition? Salespeople also run the risk of discrediting themselves when they fail to get the facts straight about competitors or their products. Architects respond to this behavior by disregarding those who speak negatively about their competition.

There is never a reason to denigrate competitors, nor is there reason to draw negative comparisons between your own products and those of your competitors. Such tactics demonstrate the fear you have about your competitors, and they usually backfire by discrediting you and possibly even enhancing the architect's interest in the competing products.

That salespeople boast of never criticizing their competitors is almost a cliché statement. Unfortunately, many salespeople fail to align this value with their behaviors. They fail to realize that they are doing just that, criticizing, when they describe all the reasons their product is better than their competitors' products. There is nothing wrong with highlighting the wonderful features of your product when making a presentation. But the presentation becomes a negative criticism when it includes statements that specifically compare your products to those of the competition.

2. **Compliment your competitor.** A wonderful way to establish credibility is to compliment your competitor. This is a great tactic for many reasons, the most important of which might be that your competitor actually produces a decent product. Many good products are on the market today, and many good people are selling them. Too often, salespeople behave in ways that suggest the only reasonable and acceptable decision for their customers is to buy from them, implying that any other decision would be a mistake.

I worked with a salesperson who would often ask his customers what other products they were considering in the decision-making process. After hearing a list of some of the competitive products from the potential customer, the salesperson was fond of saying, "Well, whatever product you choose, you're not making a mistake. Those are all good products." This statement floored and disarmed his audience every time. And it certainly had customers paying attention to what he said next. Saying this was as if he had said to them, "Hey! I have credibility, and I realize that I am not necessarily smarter than everyone else . . . But hear me out because maybe I do have something to say that would be of interest."

Your customers and prospects expect you to tell them why your product is better. They expect you to describe why your service is better and how your company is the best in the industry. You can exceed their expectations and even pleasantly surprise yourself by admitting that other high-quality companies and products are available. When you admit this to yourself and your customers, your credibility rises, and people listen more carefully to what you have to say.

3. **Stick to the agreed timeframe of your sales call.** Time is money. This is particularly true for architects, who are frequently paid by the hour. When you begin a meeting, take a few seconds to ask your audience how much time is available. You might discover that an individual is available only for a few moments. You might need to decide that you do not have enough time, based upon the answer, to conduct a credible dialogue. In this case, the professional solution is to strike interest but reschedule a meeting for a more convenient time.

Although such a brief interchange might feel like a waste of valuable time, it is a far better than irritating a customer by taking up more time than is available. You will never gain credibility if you disrespect your customer's time. A virtual law of selling and business is that nearly every meeting should stick to a predetermined timeframe. Take the initiative to establish the schedule of the meeting before it begins, and you will become respected for your efficiency.

4. **Do what you said you would do.** This seems like the simplest thing in the world to do. Yet two obstacles often prevent salespeople from fulfilling their promises—over commitment and inefficiency.

One way to fulfill this tactic is to avoid making promises you cannot keep. Salespeople eagerly commit to promises they believe will impress demanding customers. Sometimes you commit to more than you are able to accomplish and thereby destroy the credible impression you were hoping to make. The solution is to admit as quickly as possible when you will not be able to fulfill a request or a demand. Provide alternative solutions, or even explain why you are unable to fulfill a customer's demand. It's better to reduce expectations than to leave false expectations that you ultimately cannot fulfill.

The other obstacle to keeping your word is inefficiency. In other words, you forget to do what you promised. You can fulfill your commitments by simply writing down promises at the time you make them (see tactic #10—Take

Notes). Many businesspeople commonly make notes in a variety of locations—their daily planner, a notebook, a sticky note—only to later discover that they have lost an important piece of information. Write your promises down in the same place every time, and you will be likely to fulfill them promptly.

Another source of inefficiency is our own self-criticism. When we delay in fulfilling our obligations, we frequently become self-critical and depressed. Instead, we need to forgive ourselves and simply move forward. It is never too late to fulfill our promises. We live in a hectic world full of pressures and challenges to our time commitments. Most people recognize this difficulty and are sympathetic to obstacles created by time pressure.

Even if you think it is too late, stick to your word, and complete the task; you will feel happier for the experience. But if you do not eventually fulfill promises, everyone loses. Failure to fulfill a promise is the quickest way to destroy your credibility balloon. Better late than never—if you failed to fulfill a commitment in a timely way, apologize, and then do what you said you would do. Be gentle with yourself by remembering it is never too late to fulfill a commitment. This approach is a sure-fire way to protect your credibility.

5. **Educate your customers about your products in a general way.** The Tile Lady was never intent on creating a sales pitch solely focused on her products. Instead, she continually let her customers know as much as she could about the happenings in her segment of the industry. In this way, they relied on her as a credible resource for all products in her industry category. You can accomplish the same credibility by teaching your customers about all the various technologies and innovations that are occurring in your industry category. The AIA provides the perfect vehicle to help you in this endeavor, through the CES (Continuing Education System) program for continuing education. AIA members are required, as a condition of their licensing and membership to earn 30 continuing education credits annually. As a product supplier, you may be eligible to provide some off those credits with education programs and event sponsorships. Consult with your local chapters for more details about becoming an accredited provider of continuing-education credits. If you can establish your credentials as an expert in your industry category, you will become the first person architects contact when they need technical assistance.

A box-lunch program provides a wonderful opportunity to introduce a group of architects to the capabilities that *you possess as an industry expert*. The objective that most salespeople have when they present to a group of architects is to take advantage of a captive audience to deliver a one-hour sales pitch. This objective may be offensive to the architects if they chose to attend the session to improve their industry knowledge. Focusing on a loftier objective, positioning yourself as an industry expert, will go a long way toward enhancing your credibility.

One of the most powerful ways you can distinguish your credibility and skill is to educate architects about common product features in your industry that nobody else is talking about. When I was in the market for a new car, for example, the automobile salesman described "unique" safety features of his automobile brand. He described in detail how bumpers implode, and how the bolts of seatbelts and seats are engineered and tested to ensure that the seat doesn't go flying out the windshield while the airbag is popping in my face. He explained how the crumple zones in the frame and body components of the car absorb impact so that my fragile body will not. The safety features he described to me were fascinating and, I later discovered, hardly unique to his brand of auto. In fact, the safety features he described were legally required in all cars sold anywhere in the country. Yet his explanation went a long way toward establishing his credibility, in spite of the fact that the features were hardly unique to his product.

You can establish the same credibility by describing unique industry features relative to your product, such as installation details, mandatory legal specifications, and manufacturing processes. Educate architects to empower them and establish your credibility.

6. **Present the innovations of your company.** You will be most influential when you show architects how your products are uniquely distinguished from those of your competitors. You must be able to fulfill the previous tactic (i.e., provide an education about your industry in general), but it is imperative that you skillfully describe the *innovative* options and features of *your* product and service. You are responsible for educating architects on the evolution of products in the industry, with your products playing a key role in that evolution. Imagine the embarrassment architects would feel if their clients possessed a stronger knowledge of the latest industry innovations than they did. Present these innovations and options professionally to increase sales opportunities and credibility while you give them more power in their design decisions.

7. **Volunteer the limitations of your own product and service.** Nobody is perfect, and yet we fear exposing our own weaknesses and vulnerabilities. Problems arise in business relationships when we fail to disclose reality. If we do not prepare architects for the limitations of our abilities, then we are setting ourselves up for certain failure. If we permit expectations of architects and customers to remain unchecked, we place everyone in situations in which we cannot possibly fulfill unrealistic expectations. The result will be negative emotions that diminish our credibility, sales opportunities, and business relationships. Tom, the vice president of sales for a manufacturer of windows and millwork, commonly states to new customers, "I truly hope something goes wrong on one of the first orders you place with my company. You will quickly discover how well we respond to service challenges." This powerful statement prepares customers for the reality that nobody is perfect and makes a proud boast about a real feature of the company—excellent after-sale service.

Salespeople are fond of making bold statements about their product capabilities and company performance, particularly with architects. Many salespeople have stated, "If you draw it, we can build it." I have heard this said dozens of times in my career, and I cringe every time. There is no reason to make a false claim that sets you up for certain failure. There are always limitations to manufacturing capabilities. If you do not limit the expectations of architects, you may soon discover that they create a design you cannot fulfill, thus destroying your credibility. Prepare architects by volunteering the limitations of your capabilities.

8. Send thank-you notes. One of the easiest ways you can distinguish yourself from competitors is to offer a note of thanks. No hard and fast rules tell you when to write thank-you notes. If you make a habit of sending them to clients, prospects, friends, and family regularly, you might discover that you impress the most important person in your life—yourself. Mailing thank-you notes feels good and creates wonderful karma and good will. Send thank-you notes to improve more than your credibility. Send thank-you notes because you will become happier for the experience. There is no substitute for good manners.

9. Drink water and eat mints. This little reminder hopefully will help the minority of salespeople who quickly destroy all chances for short-term success by offending customers with bad breath or other poor hygiene. A lack of water can create bad breath. Water will help cleanse your breath and enhance your health. Parsley also is a natural breath freshener and delicious to boot. Eat a breath mint or the parsley garnish after lunch, and avoid suffering any embarrassment that will damage your image and credibility.

On a related note, study conducted many years ago at the University of Southern California concluded that the most important factor of influence in a conversation is the speaker's appearance. The study concluded that 57 percent of your impact during a presentation is a result of your physical appearance. You have often heard the phrase, "It's not what you say, it's how you say it . . ." The USC study concluded that 36 percent of your message is absorbed by how you say the words, while only 7 percent of the impact of your message is to the result of the words you actually use. Check your appearance by brushing your hair and teeth. Drink water and eat a mint to ensure that you are giving yourself the competitive edge.

10. Take notes! You may not believe this, but hundreds of salespeople believe taking notes is rude. This debate has occurred dozens of times at seminars. The conclusion we nearly always agree upon is that it is impossible to remember every minute detail of a conversation. We have additionally discovered that most people do not remember many of the important, broad-stroke issues shortly after a meeting has occurred. It is hardly unusual for salespeople to have up to 10 meetings in a day with various customers, prospects, and architects. There is no way they can remember every comment or commitment made in all those meetings at the conclusion of the day—unless they have taken notes during the meetings.

One common claim made during our seminar debates is that many salespeople wait until they get back to their car to write down the notes from a meeting. During a coaching session I had with a salesperson, he stated that this was his credo: "Keep it casual; don't take notes in front of the client." He asserted that taking notes indicated that he was not listening carefully to the customer. As we sat in a meeting with an executive vice president who was referring us to the regional purchasing agent, the VP pulled out his Rolodex and recited the phone number and address of this key contact to meet within his company. The salesperson I was with had to watch helplessly as I wrote down this valuable information. When we returned to his car, he asked me for the information, which left me to wonder how he would have handled the situation had I not attended the meeting with him. He hadn't even brought a pen or pencil into the meeting. Sadly, this is not a rare occurrence.

If you have any concerns that you might be displaying a lack of courtesy by taking notes, simply ask your clients whether they mind your writing down a note or two during the meeting. You will discover that they link your professionalism to the attention to detail that you demonstrate. You may have a great memory, but why risk forgetting even one important detail? Take notes to ensure the growth of your credibility.

Final Word

It should be obvious that the strategies and tactics of this section will work equally well with builders. And you will discover that these tactics are effective with dealers, as well. In fact, you are probably recognizing that all of the strategies and tactics within the book have merit for a variety of audiences.

CHAPTER SIX

DEALER
SALES STRATEGIES

The relationship that exists between the dealer and manufacturer is unique. When a manufacturer opens multiple dealerships in a market, competition between those dealers creates tension. Dealer salespeople can freely sell to any builder or architect in the marketplace with the confidence that they are contributing in no way to competition between builders. Builders may squawk occasionally, but rarely would they sever a business relationship because a competing builder purchased from the same dealer as they buy from. In contrast, a dealer's decision to conduct business with a manufacturer is strongly influenced by the manufacturer's relationship with other dealers in the market. A dealer who promotes only one brand of material becomes resentful when a competing dealer of the same brand engages in price-cutting competition that threatens profitability. Thus, manufacturer representatives must achieve a delicate balance in which the manufacturer's objectives are met without creating resentment within a dealer network.

Manufacturers' and dealers' objectives are often incongruous. Manufacturers strive to gain a share of the marketplace, which is usually targeted as a percentage of the total opportunity. If a manufacturer discovers that a sole dealer in a given market cannot single-handedly obtain the desired market share, the manufacturer may be justified in the pursuit of multiple dealers.

At the same time, when a dealer discovers that price competition over the same brand cuts into profitability, the dealer's resentment is sometimes justifiable. The challenge for the manufacturer is to reach a balance that satisfies each dealer's objectives and achieves the manufacturer's market-share goals.

The incongruity of needs and their mutual dependence creates a uniquely symbiotic relationship between manufacturers and dealers. Although business transactions often involve a winner and a loser, both parties in a manufacture-dealer relationship must rely on each other to successfully market and service a product brand together. If a product is not accepted in the market, everyone loses. For a successful relationship to develop between manufacturers and dealers, the relationship must be win-win and therefore requires cooperation in sales, marketing, inventory, production, and service. Manufacturers are striving to generate brand awareness and market objectives, and if they have no other products in their arsenal, they are reliant on the sales and marketing commitment of their dealer network. Dealers must choose among many manufacturers; when dealers are committed to a particular brand, they have an investment in resources that makes rapid changes difficult. This commitment creates a mutual reliance in which both dealers and manufacturers are intertwined. The relationship requires time to develop and therefore requires that both parties are committed to the success of the relationship. Thus, manufacturer representatives are selling much more than a product. They are selling a *commitment* to an entire program.

The Promotional Sales Role

The promotional sales role, unlike the transactional nature of the project sales role, is one in which salespeople are selling an ongoing commitment to a program. The role of manufacturer representatives as promotional salespeople is evident when it is compared to the other sales positions listed in Figure 6.1. Yet there are times when all salespeople should be aware of their role as promotional sales representatives. *Salespeople become promotional sales representatives whenever they are placed in a situation in which the customer*

FIGURE 6.1 Promotional Sales Roles

Manufacturer Sales Representative → Dealer

Manufacturer Sales Representative → Two-Step Distributor

Two-Step Distributor Sales Representative → Dealer

Dealer → Builder

becomes a reseller of their product. Manufacturer representatives are obviously in this role because they frequently are selling to two-step distributors and dealers, entities that resell the manufacturer's product. Two-step-distributor salespeople are usually in the promotional role for the same reasons. In truth, most sales representatives alternate between roles.

Even dealer salespeople will find themselves in a promotional sales role when their customers are required to resell the value of the product. Promotional sales skills are required when builders or architects use showroom displays, samples, literature, and technical data to resell the product. Promotional sales skills are required whenever a customer has salespeople who resell the product. The project sales role is a transactional role in which success is measured by the completion of a single transaction. The promotional sales role is not measured by any one individual transaction, but rather by a pattern of long-term success with ongoing transactions and sales growth. Every ambitious sales professional should recognize the importance of promotional sales skills. If you want to achieve long-term success and happiness in your career, you must be able to offer tangible personal value that merits strong commitments from your customers. Promotional sales representatives are those who measure success by the commitment they are able to garner from customers.

Sales Strategies to the Reseller

Many manufacturer-dealer relationships start as a single transaction that conveniently results from an innocent request. For example, a builder approaches a dealer and names the specific brand of product he or she needs. The dealer happily contacts the manufacturer to satisfy the builder. The manufacturer acquiesces to the pressure from the dealer for pricing information, and thus the business "relationship" begins. The problem with this scenario is that there really is no relationship. There is only a single transaction, and, moreover, the dealer likely will remain on the books of the manufacturer for many years to come. Therefore, it is important to carefully structure the initial transactions of such a new relationship. The initial transactions will lay the groundwork for the future structure of the business-to-business relationship. A single, short-term transaction is no guarantee of a long-term relationship opportunity.

This type of sales behavior is a price list-and-pray tactic, a variation on the bid-and-pray tactic with builders. Manufacturer representatives, having only received feature-benefit sales training, often fail to develop the full range of sales skills required for success. They end up managing distribution channels poorly because they are not focused on commitments from customers. They assume they will achieve success merely by providing pricing information to new customers. The implication is that a single transaction will result in an ongoing relationship. Thus, they pursue customers with the objective of exchanging a credit application for a price list. They are later surprised to discover that they have "signed up" many new customers but have failed to achieve significant sales growth.

Case Study

Two competing wood-window manufacturers have vastly different distribution philosophies. One manufacturer has a large sales force that is unregulated in its behaviors and selection of dealers. The manufacturer has nearly 3,000 dealers throughout the country. The manufacturer's competitor is a manufacturer with fewer than 100 dealers throughout the country. The manufacturer with 100 dealers outsells the other manufacturer by a factor of more than 4 to 1. It is obvious that opening up thousands of uncommitted dealers is no substitute for careful selection of a few committed dealers.

The Good Strategy—Gain Commitments

> STRATEGY #5:
>
> Gain commitments from dealers
> *before* consummating the relationship.

The challenge of earning dealer commitments begins with the task of defining "acceptable" commitment levels. Ideally, manufacturers would like their dealers to focus all of their efforts on the manufacturers' products. Committed dealers, in the eyes of manufacturers, are those who devote maximum resources to sales, service, marketing, training, promotion, planning, and growth. Committed dealers are unflagging in their loyalty, devotion, and commitment to the chosen manufacturers. Dealers, alternatively, resist commitment to any single brand of product. Dealers seek manufacturers who promote the brand to create easy sales for the dealers. Ideal manufacturers are those who develop a brand that builders, architects, and consumers request by name. Dealers merely need to take orders and enjoy the resulting profits. The objectives of manufacturers and dealers are so obviously dissonant that it is a wonder strong, committed, long-term relationships evolve at all.

Dealers deserve better than manufacturers who place no value on the loyalty of their dealers. Dealers have bills to pay, and competitive challenges; and they often are forced to operate on slim margins. Manufacturers deserve better than dealers who expect manufacturers to do all the work. Manufacturers often invest millions of dollars in advertising, marketing tools, service support, product research, and product development. Manufacturers would seemingly be entitled to dealers who offer some modicum of loyalty and marketing effort. More than a price list must bind manufacturers and dealers. There must be mutual commitment.

A critical issue for salespeople, probably the most misunderstood, is that such commitments can be made only by the leadership of the dealer. Even when dealer salespeople want a product, they will have a difficult time fulfilling sales commitments without the support of the dealer's leadership. And although purchasing agents and salespeople are often influential in sales and marketing decisions, the sales leadership, whether represented by the owner, a vice president, or a sales-management team, is ultimately responsible for investments and commitments to showrooms, sales accountability, training, and marketing.

---

10 TACTICS THAT GAIN STRONG COMMITMENT

1. Determine product sales capabilities.
2. Recognize when a committed product specialist is necessary.
3. Agree on showroom displays.
4. Establish advertising commitments.
5. Know the organizational flowchart.
6. Establish a training agenda.
7. Verify commitments in writing.
8. Generate enthusiasm.
9. Listen for areas of concern.
10. Satisfy areas of concern, without overselling.

Gaining Strong Commitment

Here are 10 tactics that will help ensure that you gain strong commitment from your customers:

1. **Determine product sales capabilities.** A national distributor of windows and vinyl siding once purchased a Chicago window dealer for whom I worked. When the parent company purchased our dealership, it expected to capitalize on a highly successful window sales operation. The parent company expected to capitalize on the good will between the dealership and its customers by successfully adding vinyl siding to the product mix. The parent company surmised that, because many of its other dealers throughout the country were successful selling both windows and vinyl siding, duplicating the success in a situation in which a profitable window dealer already existed would be a natural progression. Unfortunately, the success of the venture was contingent upon much more than the good will of the customers and a two-day product (feature-benefit) training seminar for the salespeople.

The customers who were purchasing both windows and vinyl siding at the distributor's dealerships throughout the country were primarily remodeling contractors. The types of customers with whom we dealt at the window dealership were largely tract home builders. These builders had successful business relationships with siding installers and never directly purchased vinyl siding; instead, they relied on installers to obtain materials. The installers were purchasing materials from other dealers in our market. Our sales force would have been forced to sell to a whole new audience, the siding installers, if we were to generate success with our existing customer base. The dealership never successfully made the conversion to vinyl-siding sales. The sales structure of the dealership was not compatible with the implementation of a vinyl-siding program.

This situation reflects the challenge manufacturers face. The example is particularly poignant because, in spite of the parent company's ownership and power over our dealership, the program failed.

As a promotional salesperson, you must investigate and verify your customer's ability and desire to resell the product. Among many factors, the most relevant issues to investigate include the following:

- The customer's sales structure
- The customer base
- Product compatibility
- Capital equipment needs
- The sales desire

The customer's sales structure can be evaluated both quantitatively and qualitatively. Salespeople's ability and time are limited. Thus, one can predict the sales capacity for any particular sales team. If a promotional sales representative sets a sales goal of $1,000,000 and expects that a sales force of two individuals will achieve the goal, then the sales representative had better know whether each of the salespeople can average $500,000.

Qualitative measurement issues obviously have an impact on the promotional salesperson's evaluation. The expertise and willingness of the sales team will help determine whether estimates of sales volume should be aggressive or conservative. The best predictor of future performance is past behavior. If an organization has a track record for successful implementation of new products, then sales projections can be aggressive.

The reseller's customer base is also a critical factor to evaluate. Determining when a dealer has a ready-made audience for the promotional salesperson's products is important. In the example above, when the national distributor of siding and windows purchased the local window dealer, the distributor failed to recognize the unsuitability of the customer base. The dealer's customer base of tract builders did not contain the siding installers and remodelers that would ensure success. A promotional sales representative should know who the specific target audience is for his or her products—e.g., tract builder, remodeler, custom-home builder, and installer—and ensure that the reseller of the products is capable of addressing that audience.

Product compatibility, therefore, becomes an important criterion. For example, cabinets and windows sell well together because the products are both part of the millwork family *and* are sold to the same audience, the builder. Roofing and windows often fail to work well together because, although they are both parts of the exterior "envelope" of the home, they are sold to different audiences. Roofing installers work in crews that usually focus on the installation of one product, shingles. Many roofing suppliers who claim success with their window division still admit that the windows are often less than 10 percent of their total organization sales. Even this 10 percent success is typically based on a commitment to market the windows to a separate type of customer, often with a separate sales force. Successful relationships between manufacturers and dealers are enhanced when the various products sold are a good fit with each other.

A reseller of products needs to possess the capital equipment—trucks, warehouse, and so on—to successfully service customer needs. If a dealer is lacking the proper capital equipment and unwilling to make the necessary investment, that dealer will not be a good candidate for the manufacturer. If a dealer owns only flatbeds, the dealer might need to invest in covered trucks that can safely preserve vulnerable materials during delivery. A dealer with limited storage space may not be able to support required inventory levels. These are all issues that should be resolved before the relationship commences.

In the end, even when all indicators point toward success, salespeople's resistance to change is enough to destroy the success of a relationship. A salesperson who has commonly sold commodity products such as lumber or drywall may not have the patience required to sweat the details necessary for success in a specialty product such as cabinets or windows. Even when a dealer is committed to the success of the relationship with the manufacturer, a highly skilled manufacturer representative will recognize whether and when the sales force is prepared to support a program.

Case Study

Lee, a successful "old-timer" in the window business, took advantage of a unique feature of his product to open various dealers in his market. Unfortunately, he failed to get the requisite commitments from key dealers before he started the business relationships. His company offered the unique feature of hardwood species on the interior of a designer-grade window. Lee's primary competitor had a strong relationship with a large-volume window dealer. The dealer, however, was extremely interested in Lee's product for one reason— the hardwood species. The dealer made no promises of commitment to Lee's product except for the expressed interest in the hardwood species. Lee offered his product line to the dealer, and predicted that the dealer's sales would grow and that Lee's manufacturer would eventually replace the volume of business currently enjoyed by his competitor. Despite advice from numerous peers and supervisors to withhold the product until a stronger commitment could be garnered from the dealer, Lee moved forward. His behavior, in spite of his protestations to the contrary, represented price list-and-pray tactics. Ten years later, his competitor enjoys a relationship worth more than $5 million in business, while Lee's company sells less than $200,000 of a nearly identical product. Lee's company is used to provide only the few unique products that his competitor does not offer. Lee's problems are further aggravated by the fact that the dealer continues to receive product updates and competitive information from him, which makes it very easy for the dealer to compete against Lee's more committed customers! Lee stopped working for the company, and, seven years after his departure, nothing has changed to improve the relationship. Threats by the manufacturer to sever the relationship would destroy any future potential that might still exist. Continuing the relationship hurts the manufacturer in the ways already described. The opportunity for a solution to this challenge passed many years ago when the relationship started on the wrong footing. Asking for a stronger commitment after a relationship has been consummated is extremely difficult.

2. **Recognize when a committed product specialist is necessary.** When a promotional salesperson is selling a product to a company that is very familiar with the product category, neither special product training nor a product specialist is required to properly support the sales effort. But when the company is completely unfamiliar with the product category, then a committed product specialist might be needed.

The cabinet industry has created the designation of a specialist who helps dealerships adapt to special product knowledge and sales challenges—the *CKD*, or *Certified Kitchen Designer*. Specialized kitchen distributors commonly sell kitchen cabinets. A cabinet manufacturer who partners with a dealer recognizes the need for such a product specialist. The product specialist is needed to answer specific questions regarding the details of a project order. The details required to properly price and order cabinets mandate that a product specialist is available at all times, to ensure that administrative tasks flow smoothly.

A product specialist is unnecessary in situations in which the dealer (or reseller) is an organization whose entire staff concentrates solely on the product category. For example, numerous dealers throughout the country specialize in the sale of windows and doors. A manufacturer representative would not expect a product specialist to be necessary in this situation.

The error promotional salespeople commonly make is that they limit their target sales audience. Salespeople who become overly focused on the pursuit of dealers who are already selling products in their category may miss the opportunity to introduce a completely new sales division to a dealer. Highly skilled promotional sales representatives recognize that some of their best prospects have never sold the manufacturer's type of product before. The opportunity is there for manufacturer representatives to help dealers build a whole new business division. For example, home-improvement roofing installers might be great candidates for vinyl-siding products because they have a ready network of satisfied customers to whom they can market a new product.

Case Study

Bob, a regional manager for a prominent window manufacturer, worked diligently with a dealer of kitchen cabinets in the Midwest. The dealer had a very successful operation, with seven locations throughout Michigan and Ohio. When Bob approached the dealer about the idea of entering the windows business, the dealer was very interested. The dealer concluded that existing cabinet customers would be the same people to purchase windows. The vice president of sales realized that the dealer had reached the peak of its market share for cabinets and would need to create a catalyst if the company wanted to continue its growth. Most salespeople would have jumped at the chance to immediately give the dealer a price list, samples, and a few showroom displays. Bob recognized, however, that success would be predicated on the dealer's ability to manage a whole new product line. Doing this would require that a window specialist be hired and trained for each location. Bob took the time to ensure that his new dealer would be willing to invest in the personnel to successfully launch this new product. Bob reported that the dealer sold "only two million dollars" of windows in the first year, but the foundation of his program created a structure that resulted in a long-term relationship that has now lasted nearly a decade.

---

3. **Agree on showroom displays.** As a stipulation to the distribution agreement, manufacturers often require dealers to install showroom displays. Nevertheless, dealers frequently discover ways to avoid displaying product or to "bury" displays in nondescript locations. When resellers agree to take advantage of displays, always gain commitments regarding how the displays will be used. Some products require showroom displays to achieve status in the market, while others sell successfully using portable hand samples. The promotional sales representative should determine the necessity of showroom displays and seek the appropriate commitments from resellers.

Because a showroom display is not always essential to the success of a program, you should be prepared to accept when dealers opt out of the display program. The best indicator of need is based on the reseller's current practices. If the reseller has minimal showroom exposure, then a display may not be necessary. Many leading suppliers of lumber and millwork are successful in spite of the absence of a fancy showroom. If a customer's commitment to various product brands includes showroom displays, then you should ensure that your customers agree to display products *before* you consummate the relationship.

4. **Establish advertising commitments.** Most manufacturers seek dealers who develop local advertising campaigns to cultivate brand awareness for the manufacturer-dealer partnership. The manufacturers encourage the development of these programs by offering co-op advertising allowances, but these allowances frequently become a source of tension and combative negotiation. Dealers want their suppliers to simply "give" them the money to use in any way the dealers deem appropriate, whereas manufacturers want to exercise paternalistic control over the allocation of the funds. Numerous manufacturers are making their co-op programs more successful by reducing the red tape. Conversely, many dealers are becoming more sophisticated in their use of advertising funds and are acquiescing to manufacturer's expectations.

Once again, highly skilled sales representatives recognize that a key component of the promotional sales role is to establish an understanding and commitment to marketing and advertising programs *before* the relationship is consummated. The discussion of advertising and promotion should be on the program agenda checklist for every salesperson in a promotional sales role. Even in the absence of a co-op advertising agreement, strong dealers in the marketplace should be able to describe their marketing vision and advertising methods. If you are working with a dealer who is unwilling to match the marketing and advertising challenge of the competing dealers in his or her marketplace, that is a sign that other dealers might be better candidates for your products.

5. **Know the organizational flowchart.** When the timing is appropriate, promotional sales representatives should clarify the roles of relevant employees within the customer's organization. Many salespeople discover these details gradually after the sale has been made. Getting this information up front can gain valuable time, and the process of building relationships with key individuals can begin quickly. Doing this can establish sales momentum early and help to launch an exciting new relationship when numerous people within the organization feel connected to the process. Skilled promotional sales representatives take time to understand, as much as their dealers will allow, the work processes and personnel flowchart of their customers. Understanding organizational flowcharts will help determine who needs training.

6. **Establish a training agenda.** In spite of previous comments to the contrary, feature-benefit product training plays an important role in the development of a successful promotional sales campaign. The previous comments were offered to emphasize that feature-benefit training is merely one component of a successful supplier-customer program.

In addition to providing feature-benefit training, salespeople in their promotional role must clarify administrative procedures for product ordering and servicing. Every supplier has different methods for processing orders, and unique terminology that customers must learn. Every supplier has unique idiosyncrasies in delivery, ordering, and service policies. These policies need to be clarified. Dealers' purchasing and sales-department employees will quickly become frustrated if they discover too many mistakes occurring in the course of the burgeoning relationship.

Perhaps your employer has a formal program by which customers can receive the necessary product training, and perhaps not. Whether or not your organization offers a standard program, you should recognize that numerous efforts will be necessary to adequately train a customer. Remember that repetition is the mother of learning. Most salespeople are ill equipped with training skills. Because dealers need to absorb a lot about your company—administrative functions, product details, and product sales features, you should plan a *series* of training events, to ensure that administrative fundamentals and product details are properly explained. As sales representative, you should also plan follow-up coaching sessions with appropriate personnel during the start-up period of the business relationship. During those coaching sessions, you can lend assistance and one-on-one training to create confidence in the ordering process. Remember that the administrative training may be more important to the success of the relationship than the feature-benefit training that focuses on sales features.

After all, a company cannot successfully sell a product it does not know how to properly obtain from its supplier.

7. **Verify commitments in writing.** Verifying your conversations in writing is just as important as taking notes during meetings. The construction industry is an informal business in which many transactions are conducted with a handshake. It is also a business in which salespeople are frequently reminded of their customers' versions of previous conversations. Customers often tell salespeople about a commitment that they believe was previously promised. The perceived commitments frequently result from a lack of clarity during conversations. Customers may have made statements in meetings that salespeople did not agreed upon, but neither did they deny or correct the statements. Salespeople may have made statements that customers misconstrued. So keeping written records of conversations is a good practice for salespeople. Likewise, it is an excellent practice for salespeople to write follow-up letters after meetings to verify details of conversations and commitments that were made (or were not made) on both parties' behalf. Even if confusion arises later, at least customers will recognize that the confusion is not necessarily the complete fault of the salespeople.

8. **Generate enthusiasm.** Enthusiasm is contagious, and it's a marvelous way to help launch a relationship. As obvious as it may seem, you have seen salespeople who focus their promotional sales efforts solely on sales leadership of the customer (exactly as recommended in this chapter), while they leave the customer's employees out of the excitement. This tactic is a reminder to create a plan with the customer's leadership that will generate enthusiasm among employees. Salespeople for the dealer are almost always excited about adding a new product to their arsenal, while, for the rest of the employees, a new product is merely one additional set of tasks heaped onto their existing workload. Promotional sales representatives should prepare to create excitement for all of their customers' personnel.

Many salespeople rely on their customers to write memos and make plans for their employees to learn about a new product the dealer will be selling. Great salespeople help the sales-leadership team launch the new product-promotion campaign. In some cases, promotional sales representatives even request permission to handle the internal communications of the program.

As a leader for a training organization, I have frequently offered to supply my clients with memos they can distribute to their employees. My hope is to clarify program expectations and generate the enthusiasm that makes the event an exciting success for everyone involved. We should always strive to do the same as we introduce our products.

9. **Listen for areas of concern.** Ben Franklin once said, "Keep your eyes wide open before marriage, half shut afterward." In other words, *before* we actually begin the relationship, we should look out for the probability that problems will emerge later in the relationship. The nature of salespeople is

to avoid conflict because, after all, their job is to develop mutually beneficial relationships. A foreseeable area of concern may not be insurmountable but, if ignored, it might cause unnecessary tension that later will hamper the relationship.

10. **Satisfy areas of concern, without overselling.** To preserve your credibility, you may need to volunteer limitations for your company. In your effort to satisfy the other tactics in this section, numerous red flags may emerge. For example, if dealers expect you to provide an advertising allowance that requires no co-op investment from them, you must reiterate that the program requires dealer participation to become applicable. Another challenge may arise when dealers explain that they cannot provide time for employees to be properly trained on your product because it is their busy season. In this case, you might have to schedule the program startup at a time more convenient to them. Dealers who refuse to display your products in the showroom might be a deal stopper, especially if your competitor's products are on display. Satisfy areas of concern where possible and remember that, as noted earlier, No is not necessarily No. Maybe No means Not now.

The Great Strategy—Plan the Future

> STRATEGY #6:
>
> Plan the structure of the relationship.

The previous strategy concentrates on achieving commitments from dealers to participate in the programs you have to offer. This strategy focuses on ways to structure the relationship after both parties have agreed to move forward. A parent would not agree to give the car keys to a son or daughter without first agreeing on the teenager's responsibilities for maintaining and driving the vehicle. The youth would be expected to ensure cleanliness, maintenance, and proper use of the vehicle. The parent would inspect the vehicle to ensure that the commitments the son or daughter made are being followed. This section is not intended to suggest that a relationship between a manufacturer and a dealer is paternalistic in nature. In fact, this strategy helps to eliminate the common practices of manufacturers behaving in a way that suggests a paternal relationship exists. A son or daughter who agrees to the parameters of the automobile maintenance requirements merits respect as an adult. A parent who neglects to ensure that a fair agreement exists merits no more respect than a child. The relationship between a manufacturer and dealer should involve two mature organizations that are willing to adhere to the parameters of their agreement.

In our industry, leading manufacturers have methods in place to ensure that their dealers participate in the various marketing and sales programs. The leading manufacturers wield enough clout to enforce the participation in those programs. Conversely, many manufacturers have defined dealer programs on paper, but they fail to make those programs materialize in actuality. For companies that already have institutionalized programs, the following tactics will help them strengthen those programs and gain insight for new ideas. This text provides a training tool by which their sales representatives can become more effective at structuring business relationships. For the many manufacturers who are still striving to strengthen their dealer marketing commitments, the strategies and tactics of this chapter provide guidelines to help their salespeople bring their programs to fruition.

---

10 TACTICS THAT STRUCTURE THE RELATIONSHIP

1. Define your role in the relationship.
2. Know your market-share goals.
3. Enlist the dealer's support for your market-share goals.
4. Create sales goals.
5. Plan sales events.
6. Define service responsibilities.
7. Plan future communication with sales leadership.
8. Put the plan in writing.
9. Gain commitment from leaders in the organization.
10. Know when to end the relationship.

Structuring the Relationship

Use the methods outlined in the tactics that follow to more effectively structure your business relationships with your customers:

1. **Define your role in the relationship.** The salesperson is, or at least should be, the main point of contact in a manufacture-dealer relationship. The salesperson's manager is often involved in the commitment phase of the sale and hopefully ends his or her involvement at that point; deferring maintenance responsibilities to the salesperson after the relationship is consummated. A sales manager who continually acts as the point of contact after the relationship has begun is a sales manager who has too much time on his or her hands. The sales manager should be performing as a coach and supporter of the salesperson, not as the hero who steps in daily to perform the salesperson's job. But that is a subject for a different book.

Once the relationship has begun, the customer should fully understand the role of the salesperson. All too often a salesperson in a promotional role is at a loss to define what benefit he or she can provide the customer. A salesperson without a vision will soon be lost. As a wise philosopher once said, "If you don't know where you're going, any road will get you there." The salesperson's vision should include a sincere desire to generate sales and profits for the customer by actively engaging in sales, marketing, event planning, training, and any other activities that will create confidence for the dealer's personnel.

The salesperson should also clarify the limitations of his or her abilities and willingness to perform specific tasks. For example, a manufacturer representative is often called upon to provide take-offs from blueprints, or to repair defective products. These may be tasks that the salesperson assumes are the dealer's responsibility. Such issues should be clarified before the relationship begins. If you delineate your responsibilities in the relationship and ensure that your customer agrees, you avoid the future stress of always being called to handle issues for which you have neither the ability nor the time to perform.

2. **Know your market-share goals.** This tactic seems so obvious that it is not worth mentioning, yet it might be the single most-overlooked aspect of manufacturer sales values and behaviors. Dale, a Montana sales representative for a window manufacturer, sold $4.8 million worth of windows in a state of 800,000 people, an astounding market share of $6 per person for a company that sold less than $1 per person nationally. The following year, his sales dropped by $300,000. A casual observer might conclude that Dale's magic had worn off. Upon closer inspection of his territory, however, one would have discovered that housing starts had dropped off more than 10 percent. Rather than consider that Dale had lost sales volume, one could assert that he actually had gained market share. It would have been fair to expect that the sales of someone who had already successfully saturated a market would mirror the trends in the market, not to mention the likelihood that he would lose sales ground simply because he was a major target for his competitors. But Dale's loss of 6.25 percent was a successful performance during a year in which housing starts dropped by 10 percent. In other words, in spite of decreasing sales, Dale had actually increased his market share! If you agree that Dale had a successful year, then you would have to agree that market-share goals are an essential measurement of performance.

Employers usually measure the performance of their sales representatives based upon sales volume and margin dollars. But measuring sales performance relative to market trends is also an important indicator of success. Achieving sales growth is always good, although the results can sometimes be misleading. A salesperson with steady sales in a severely soft market might be performing better than a salesperson with very slight increases in a hot market. So define your market-share goals to create the foundation upon which you can measure the success of your total dealer network.

3. **Enlist the dealer's support for your market-share goals.** Market-share goals become important measurements of relative success and also an excellent tool to enlist the support of your dealers. As noted earlier, combative dealers commonly request arrangements in which they are exclusive dealers of product brands in defined markets. A skillful manufacturer representative focuses on market-share objectives as a measurement of success.

When a dealer requests exclusive or semi-exclusive arrangements, the skilled manufacturer representative quickly enlists the support of the combative negotiator by focusing the discussion on market-share objectives.

The first step in the discussion about market-share goals requires that you gain agreement, or at least an understanding, from the sales leadership of the dealer about *your* market-share goals. Your goals may not be the same as the dealer's goals. It is, nevertheless, important that the dealer understand your goals. If a salesperson can help a dealer see the reasonable point of view of the manufacturer, then the dealer is left with no choice but to recognize that a fair share of the market is what any credible business partner should be seeking. If the salesperson is focused on a (realistic) target share of the market, the negotiation becomes simple. The salesperson merely needs to state what the target share is and then ask what percentage of that the dealer can create. When the dealer proudly boasts that he or she will provide the entire share, then the salesperson should shift the conversation to the methods by which the dealer will achieve the goals. It *is* possible that a single dealer would be able to achieve the market-share objective of the manufacturer, although it is more often the case that a manufacturer will need to open up numerous dealers in any given market. The only way to know whether more than one dealer is required is to develop acute goal-setting skills by which the salesperson can accurately predict future performance.

4. Create sales goals. The ability to create sales goals is often overshadowed by the ability to make boastful promises. Manufacturers consistently request "budgets" from their salespeople within which the manufacturers expect an assurance of sales growth. But many such "projections" are little more than boastful goals based on sparse data carelessly accumulated.

Salespeople can obtain accurate projections of future performance only when they consider a variety of factors. Sales goals should consider factors such as market conditions, target volume, market share, closing ratios, attrition of existing business, and the performances of individual dealer accounts and salespeople. When the promotional sales representatives meet with their resellers, they should be able to understand the details by which the dealers establish and monitor the goals for various products.

An integral component of the goal-setting process is the involvement of customer projections. For example, after you have shared your overall sales goals with customers, you should discuss what level of volume those customers can provide toward that goal. Keep in mind that it is within their interest to project both aggressively and accurately. An aggressive goal ensures that you will need to open fewer dealers, much to each dealer's benefit. An aggressive goal also ensures that each dealer will earn your constant attention. Accurate goals stabilize relationships by creating dependability between suppliers and customers. A skilled salesperson can cross-reference various goals to make sure things add up properly. For example, the sales-volume goals of individual salespeople should equal the total goal of the dealer. The sales-volume goals of individual dealers should nearly equal the total goal for the market. Set individual goals with your resellers to enhance communication in the relationship.

5. **Plan sales events.** You can plan any of a multitude of events with customers-trade shows, golf outings, breakfast presentations, dinner events, and so on-to generate excitement and sales opportunities. The success of a sales event is dependent on the long-term opportunity that the event creates. Thus, every sales event that you plan should account for ongoing follow up after the program is complete. The objective of a sales event is nothing more than a massive prospecting campaign. The biggest mistake salespeople make is to sponsor a sales event and assume that the purpose of the event is the event itself. In the aftermath of an event based on this assumption, all that has been accomplished is some activity with minimal future benefit.

Manufacturers and dealers often engage in *sales "blitzes,"* events in which a group of salespeople target a geographic area with intensive prospecting efforts. At the conclusion of the event, congratulations are offered, awards are given, and everyone returns home a winner, or so they think. But the event is not a success just because the activity has been completed. The event will be a success if sales are generated. One unique way you can distinguish yourself from other salespeople is to create long-term benefit from sales events.

An event merely introduces you to new prospects (or keeps you in front of existing ones) and sets the stage for future activity. Plan your event by carefully selecting the target audience. Then enlist the participation of people who stand to gain from the long-term growth in business you anticipate. Finally, plan your ongoing follow-up for every person who attended the event. Measure your success for the long term, not by the number of people you saw on the day of the event. You would rather gain 5 long-term customers from only 20 event prospects than 1 long-term customer from 100 event prospects. The goal is long-term productivity and sales success, not activity.

6. **Define service responsibilities.** One area of confusion between manufacturers and dealers often revolves around service responsibilities. Dealers invariably *assume* that the manufacturer will handle all after-sale service complaints. Thus, the conversation about service never occurs. The manufacturer representative should instigate this dreaded conversation to discuss the policies regarding service arrangements and thus ensure good will in the market. Nothing will turn off a builder faster than a frustrating experience in which a dealer and manufacturer stand around pointing fingers at each other while the builder suffers.

7. **Plan future communication with sales leadership.** Most manufacturer representatives invest a significant portion of their time schmoozing with the top brass at the dealership. Doing this is often an important function of the position, but frequently it is not necessary. Some business lead-

ers do not need the attention that salespeople persistently provide. The time manufacturer representatives invest with their customer's boss is time away from creating sales and servicing the product. A highly skilled manufacturer representative establishes a level of communication that is comfortable and efficient for both parties.

8. **Put the plan in writing** and communicate the plan face to face with the dealer. Most manufacturers have a dealer agreement or an outline of the dealer program. The program usually includes a pricing discount and additional requirements that vary, depending on a multitude of factors. The manufacturer representatives need to verify the details of the relationship in writing. In spite of manufacturers' desire to standardize the terms of their dealer agreements, most manufacturers do not wield enough clout to dictate all the parameters of the business relationship. Thus, skilled manufacturer representatives take the initiative to achieve a balance that is fair for both parties, and they verify the details in writing, including a file that they submit to the manufacturer.

9. **Gain commitment from leaders in the organization.** This tactic has been stated and implied numerous times in this chapter, but it is worth repeating. The manufacturer-dealer relationship is most successful when the sales leadership, whether represented by an individual or by consensus, is committed to the partnership. The sales-leadership team needs to support the sales goals, training, and service that contribute to the success of the relationship. The sales leadership needs to be committed to the dialogue and activities that will nurture and strengthen the relationship over time. If the leadership is not committed, then the manufacturer representative is facing an uphill battle.

10. **Know when to end the relationship.** The price list-and-pray tactic creates numerous dealers who have access to price and product information, although the dealers often generate no sales. The effect this has on the manufacturer can be troubling. At best, the manufacturer is wasting resources maintaining an account relationship that ended years earlier. At worst, the manufacturer is arming a competitor with confidential information that should be discretely controlled.

Manufacturer-dealer relationships usually are not terminated; they just fade away. In fact, this is true of dealer-builder relationships, as well. Thousands of businesses in the industry have long lists of "customers" who have purchased *zero* over a span of years. But the customers remain on the books and continue to receive product updates, and sometimes even pricing updates. When the relationship is no longer benefiting both parties, it is wise to communicate a formal change in the relationship. When the manufacturer representative does this properly, a dealer will respect the ways in which the representative is managing the market. A formal notification to end a relationship often creates an opportunity for the renewal of the manufacturer-dealer relationship, and on better terms.

Final Word

I developed the strategies and tactics presented in this chapter and the next many years ago for manufacturer representatives. I quickly discovered that sales managers and dealers also benefited significantly from the information. Dealers discovered that they could strengthen their relationships with manufacturers who adopted quality sales behaviors. Many dealers discovered that they could benefit from the strategies by employing them with resellers of their materials. The role of the promotional sales representative is thus not limited to that of manufacturer representatives, but is one that nearly any salesperson can employ.

You may be sensing that, as you read further, the strategies and tactics are becoming more challenging. You are correct in this assumption and should therefore appreciate why promotional sales can be so challenging. Although the promotional sales role is one that even someone with poor sales skills can fulfill simply by waiting for the customers' salespeople to do the selling, it is a role that, when you perform it skillfully, provides incredible security and confidence. These benefits result from the rise in your personal credibility.

CHAPTER SEVEN

SALES
MANAGEMENT STRATEGIES

Aunique luxury of manufacturer representatives is the pleasure of socializing for a living because they have the fortunate opportunity to rely on their customers' salespeople to generate business. Manufacturer representatives fall into the pattern of golfing, dining, and entertaining customers as their primary business function. They assume likeability is a key to success, and thus they rely on charm and personality to establish rapport and strong relationships with customers. It is true that customers enjoy doing business with people they like, and that strong friendships often evolve from business relationships. But the key to success is establishing a strong business relationship. If a social relationship evolves from the business relationship, that is a bonus. But the foundation of the relationship is business, not friendship.

Arthur Miller's tragic character Willie Loman epitomizes the archetypal "social" salesperson. Loman struggles toward the end of his career because he has never developed the business skills that would earn him the respect and credibility necessary to survive in a changing world. He instead becomes reliant on the good will of employers and customers. He believes his own words when he angrily exclaims, "They owe me!" This tragic character from *Death of a Salesman* portrays a reality for many salespeople who discover a dearth of skills too late in their careers.

A great personality is certainly an asset in a sales career, but it is not the foundation that creates success. Likewise, manufacturer representatives or any salespeople do not need to rely on their social skills to achieve success. The profession of selling requires the development of skills. Success results from a commitment to personal development of professional skills. Promotional sales representatives are in a unique position to develop superior sales skills and ultimately achieve sales leadership by transferring those skills to other salespeople so they too can achieve career growth.

Relationship Development Strategies

The challenge for manufacturer representatives and promotional salespeople is to figure out how to strengthen the business relationship by helping their customers achieve sales growth. These salespeople often have wasted countless hours in product-training sessions and in the offices of purchasing agents, talking about product issues, while untapped sales opportunities linger in the field. They consistently make the same strategic mistake by assuming that as long as their customers have product knowledge, they will generate sales. Thus, promotional sales representatives invest resources and energy on product presentations, product education, and product service. Their perceived sales role becomes one in which their primary responsibility is to perform as product experts.

Many salespeople who proudly admit, "If I don't know the answer, I promise that I know where to get it" have become a comical stereotype. This admission, a subconscious reaction to retain flagging credibility, is an attempt by promotional sales representatives to reinforce their role as product experts. So it should not be surprising that salespeople rarely, if ever, admit,

"If I lose the sale, I promise that I will take full responsibility for my failure." Although such an admission would be impressive, it is never offered because to admit a lack of product knowledge is acceptable, but to admit that one periodically loses a sale would be (erroneously) perceived as a full-blown admission of incompetence (see the suffering of Win-Lose Thinking in Chapter 1). For salespeople to say, "Obviously, I know where to get answers to product questions. More importantly, I can promise that I have the ability to help you make money—I consider that my main task" would be more impressive and acceptable. The latter admission would demonstrate personal acceptance of sales responsibility.

Salespeople who have often made the promise to "get answers to product questions" are probably reading the previous paragraph defensively and asserting to themselves that there is nothing wrong with admitting they might not know every answer to technical questions. Although this may be true, there is nothing impressive about the admission, either. If manufacturer representatives know where to get answers, then dealer representatives also know they can use the same resource and make a quick phone call to the manufacturer's technical-support department. Manufacturer representatives who are overly focused on product issues are rendered useless to dealer salespeople who already possess enormous and comprehensive product expertise.

To achieve legitimate sales-leadership credibility, manufacturer's representatives (and any promotional salespeople) need to establish themselves not merely as product experts, but as sales experts. It is for this reason that the terms *hunter* and *farmer* (or *gatherer*) misrepresent the skill sets required for sales success. The farmer can rely on personality and product knowledge to get by. As farmers, manufacturer representatives can comfortably make product presentations, socialize, and "put out fires," although they never have to enter the field of battle where the hunt takes place, with builders and architects.

As discussed in an earlier chapter, skilled salespeople are neither hunter nor farmer; instead, they must possess both skill sets to establish credibility with customers. Manufacturer representatives who are unable to hunt for new builders and architects lack credibility with their dealers' salespeople. A common perception among dealer salespeople is that manufacturer representatives would not perform well in dealer sales because they have never developed the fundamental hunting skills to ensure success with builders and architects. This perception is often accurate, and when it is, destroys manufacturer representatives' credibility. Their inability to hunt renders them unable to generate the sales support that creates growth, which leaves them dependent upon the efforts of their customers. Their customers quickly sense this dependency and become critical of the support from their supplier's "product expert." An overriding perception that evolves is one of manufacturer sales representatives waiting helplessly at the camp while dealer salespeople go out on the hunt and bring back the rewards.

Manufacturer representatives want to be involved in the hunt and frequently strive to "ride along" with dealer representatives on sales calls. The manufacturer representatives assume that the roles of the dealer and manufacturer are implicitly defined: The dealer sales representative provides the "in" to customers and prospects, while the manufacturer representative provides the product expertise. The manufacturer representatives fail to realize that this role is not hunting but merely more farming. The ability to find new leads places dealer sales representatives in the superior position. Manufacturer representatives' credibility is diminished by their reliance on dealers.

The problem gets worse when manufacturer representatives make presentations that do not succeed with dealers' customers. The rote feature-and-benefit monologues often do little to motivate builders and architects. Manufacturer representatives naively focus on features that are important to consumers but that are of little interest to industry professionals. Manufacturer representatives subsequently come across as naïve and out of touch. Thus, dealer salespeople become resistant to individual manufacturer representatives riding along, because they lack confidence in their presentation skills. Many manufacturer representatives fail to recognize that the opportunity to ride along with their customers' salespeople is not a right, but rather an earned privilege.

As manufacturer representatives' credibility wanes, they become increasingly desperate for reasons to generate activity. Their travel activity resembles a milk delivery run, in which they continually cycle through their territory in a predictable and monotonous way. They recognize, after all, that they are being paid to do a job and so they should do *something*. Although their objective should be to generate sales for their customers, they instead schedule meetings, or, worse yet, show up with no appointment at the office of their customers, with no purpose other than to "help." Eventually, customers of these representatives discover that they have almost no purpose for their sales meetings, and the manufacturer sales representatives' credibility sinks even further.

The good news in all this for manufacturer representatives is that they have an alternative. In fact, one way they can help their customers is to drive right pass their offices and to the offices and jobsites of potential builders and architects, on their customers' behalf. The fastest path to credibility for anyone is to prove his or her skills at a task. Promotional representatives can easily demonstrate their skills simply by bringing sales and leads to their customers. When promotional sales representatives can hunt and develop sales opportunities for their customers, their actions reveal a world of opportunity and success.

The Good Strategy—Sales Involvement

> STRATEGY #7:
>
> Get salespeople involved in
> the sale of your product.

A sales manager for a dealer often has a great number of salespeople to manage, a vast array of products, a few key accounts with whom he is personally involved, officers of the company to whom he answers, regular reports he needs to review, regular reports he needs to submit, and a host of other responsibilities. If you were that sales manager and had committed to promote a product brand by investing thousands of dollars in training, showroom displays, time, and other valuable resources, what would you expect of your manufacturer sales representative? First and foremost, you would expect the manufacturer representative to make the relationship work.

Product training is essential, but it is not enough. The manufacturer representative must form direct relationships with dealers' salespeople. The best manufacturer representatives recognize that they are "earning" their dealer representatives' sales time. Dealer sales representatives have many products to choose from, and numerous responsibilities. Their time, like that of any businessperson, is limited and valuable. Thus, manufacturer representatives must recognize that their job is essentially to make selling the manufacturer's product worth these salespeoples' time.

The dealer's sales manager can push salespeople only so far toward a specific product. Eventually, individual salespeople make the decisions regarding what products to sell. And these salespeople often take the path of least resistance. Manufacturer representatives leverage results from their ability to help other salespeople sell more products in less time. If you can help your customers sell more of

Your ability to hunt *for* your customers and *with* your customers is critical to your success as a promotional sales representative.

10 TACTICS THAT GET YOUR CUSTOMERS' SALESPEOPLE INVOLVED

1. Verify that the administrative training lessons have succeeded.
2. Make sales calls to your customers' target audience.
3. Provide project leads to salespeople.
4. Make sales calls with your customers' salespeople.
5. Make sales calls to architects.
6. Provide account leads, slowly transferring relationship management.
7. Sponsor contests to spark interest.
8. Keep your salespeople informed.
9. Use your marketing department effectively.
10. Work with inside sales support in the same manner.

your product, you will help them increase their customer base. If you help them increase their customer base, they will become more loyal to you. They will seek out your assistance and proactively respond to your sales leadership. Your success is predicated on your ability to get other salespeople involved. Your ability to hunt *for* your customers and *with* your customers is critical to your success as a promotional sales representative.

Getting Your Customers' Salespeople Involved

To effectively get your customer's salespeople involved, adopt the following tactics:

1. **Verify that the administrative training lessons have succeeded.** This tactic is vitally important to your success as a promotional sales representative. One essential difference between promotional sales and project sales is that promotional sales representatives do not manually place every order. Promotional sales representatives instead rely on the administrative abilities of their customers' salespeople to successfully place orders. Even if your customers' salespeople (and internal support staff) are confident about the features and benefits of your product, you will never achieve success unless your customers can confidently place orders with your company without your assistance.

This tactic does not describe a training function. It assumes that you have already completed basic training with your customers, but that you still need to verify that the administrative lessons have succeeded. The best way to ensure that salespeople have absorbed the training is to observe them while they are placing orders with your company. In training methodology, the successful implementation of a training lesson is called *transfer of training*. You will need to verify that your training lessons have successfully been transferred to your customers' personnel. In some cases, this may mean that you will help these salespeople place numerous orders until they are comfortable with your company and its procedures. If your customers are not comfortable ordering your product, they will not be comfortable selling your product.

2. **Make sales calls *to* your customers' target audience.** The infusion of new sales opportunities and new customers is the lifeblood of any business. You will achieve your fastest means to credibility by bringing new sales opportunities to your customers. Obviously, you will need to be careful how you go about targeting prospects during this process. If you call on your customers' potential prospects, you may create animosity for the short term. If you make calls to your customers' customers without their knowledge, you run the risk of destroying important trust for the long term. The best way to avoid suspicion is to explain the game plan to your customers. Let them know that you will be trying to bring them new business. Apologize up front about the possibility you will run into a few of their existing customers.

Assure your direct customers, the dealers, that you will mention them by name in your discussions with potential prospects.

Once you have achieved success with even a few prospects, having turned them into customers for your customers, you will overcome any tension and resistance. The quickest way to gain leverage with your customers is to demonstrate your ability to sell to their target audience. The target audience for dealers is usually builders; thus, if you work for a manufacturer, call on builders to sell them your products. The target audience for installers is builders; thus, if you work for a dealer who sells primarily to installers, call on builders to sell the value of your installer's services. The target audience for remodelers is homeowners; thus, you should follow up on sales opportunities with homeowners to help your remodelers grow their business. When you can cultivate valuable leads for your customers, you will gain leverage in the marketplace and a confidence you never had before.

The largest benefit you will create for your career in selling to your customers' customers is a boost in your credibility. Your customers will quickly recognize your sales talent. They will strive to keep you involved in their business. They will recognize that you are a valuable contributor to their organization. They may even possess a healthy fear that the time you don't spend with them may be costing them valuable opportunities. You will discover that price negotiations are reduced or eliminated, and that you have more choice when selecting customers.

Case Study

Rich is a manufacturer's sales representative in Virginia. One architect he called on recommended the use of Rich's product and suggested that Rich call the contractor. The contractor was thrilled with Rich's attention and expertise. The result was that the contractor bought $7,000 worth of materials, which a local lumberyard that Rich had been pursuing as a new dealer purchased. The purchase was the first for the lumberyard and a catalyst for the company to shift $100,000 of business to Rich from one of his competitors. The lumberyard has seven other locations in Rich's territory, all of which shifted their business to Rich's company. This "pull-through" sale of one project resulted in immense benefit for Rich, and such a sale can do the same for any promotional sales representative.

---

3. **Provide** *project* **leads to salespeople.** If you prospect with your customers' target audience, you have the ability to provide them valuable leads.

Leads are furnished to salespeople from a variety of resources—employers, suppliers, walk-ins, and so on-but none is more valuable than the one you can provide to your customer. The lead you provide comes equipped with information, momentum, and your sales support. A lead is most valuable to salespeople when they sense an opportunity for immediate success. Thus, your initial offering of sales leads must consist of more than a name and phone number for a potential customer. You might not get salespeople's attention with a name and a phone number. But you will definitely get their attention with a dollar sign.

Provide project sales leads that result in fast opportunities for your customers' salespeople. Two factors will make this tactic successful—likelihood and timing. If you consistently provide sales leads to your customers that create needless paperwork, you are contributing to the bid-and-pray tactics that salespeople strive to avoid. At least initially, focus on leads that have a high probability for sales success. If you provide excellent leads early in your burgeoning relationships with salespeople, they will take all of your leads more seriously in the long run. Your early success will therefore be contingent on your ability to track the lead until the timing is right. Salespeople may not be enthusiastic about leads that come to fruition six months down the road. But they will be very excited when they get a lead that results in instantaneous success.

Your objective is to contribute to their success. Even one or two sales leads a year can provide a significant boost to a salesperson's confidence. Focus on quality, not quantity, when you are providing sales opportunities to your customers' salespeople. This tactic is vital to your success and credibility. Every remaining tactic in this chapter will become more effective once you have proven your ability to generate sales for your customers' salespeople.

4. **Make sales calls *with* your customers' salespeople.** This tactic works *after* you have successfully accomplished the previous two tactics. Credibility is not guaranteed by the title on your business card. Credibility is earned. Actions speak louder than words; your successful action of the previous tactic establishes your credibility faster than any other method. A successful way to earn your credibility is to produce sales with the same types of customers that your customers' salespeople want. When you have proven your ability to achieve success with their audience, salespeople will be eager to make joint sales calls with you. Remember, you have no right to expect salespeople to invite you to ride along on their sales calls; that is a privilege you earn.

The common practice manufacturer and dealer salespeople follow is to delineate their roles during joint sales calls in an expected manner. When selling to a builder during a joint sales call, the dealer salesperson describes the wonderful services his company offers while the manufacturer salesperson talks about the wonderful product details. A unique method to enhance the joint sales call is to reverse the salespeople's presentation roles. For example, if Joe is the salesperson for Acme Manufacturing, and Sally is the salesperson for Accurate Distribution, a reseller of Acme, then a prospect would naturally expect each salesperson to be the spokesperson for his or her own company. The listener expects Joe to say good things about Acme, while Sally boasts of the wonderful services that her company provides. But for Joe to tout the wonderful value that Accurate Distribution brings to the table is more effective. Joe can freely state, "Acme had numerous dealers to consider in the market place. We chose Accurate because it has the best resources available in this market. Sally has attended many of our training events and has proven herself to be one of the most reliable salespeople in the industry." Shortly thereafter, Sally can offer similar boasts about Acme: "We looked at a few different products, but we settled on Acme for a variety of reasons—quality products, excellent service support, and excellent sales representation that help us effectively satisfy customers' needs." Customers and prospects expect you to say wonderful things about your own company, which creates no surprises when you fulfill expectations. But when you have choices among alternatives—i.e., when a dealer freely chooses to market a product, or a manufacturer appoints one dealer from among many choices—the authority of your presentation is dramatically enhanced. When two salespeople are effective presenters of other companies, the credibility of the presentation soars.

5. **Make sales calls to architects.** You can to lead a horse to water, but you can't make him drink. But once the horse tastes the pleasant water, it often wants more. The same can be said of salespeople who have limited experience with architects. The previous tactics recommend that promotional representatives focus sales efforts on the target audience of their customers. Although it is beneficial to help your customers' salespeople with their sales to a familiar audience, this tactic lets you help them recognize new opportunities that they never knew existed. Previous data indicated that architects prefer to work with local sales representatives who are readily available to provide instant support. Although architects want local support, this reality does not instantly change attitudes. Salespeople unfortunately remain skeptical about the benefit of architectural sales. Manufacturer representatives can overcome this skepticism by finding architects who provide tangible career benefits to their customers' salespeople.

To enlist sales support, you should carefully develop relationships, one at a time, with architects, and slowly transfer control of those relationships to your customers' salespeople. The timing is appropriate to begin transferring control of those relationships when a project sales opportunity is available with an architect. When the project approaches the bid phase, invite one of you customers' salespeople to join you in the sale of the project. The salespeople will not recognize that you may have been calling on that architect repeatedly for a period of months. You can later demonstrate the ways in which you treated that architect as a paying customer. Your initial transfer of the relationship should involve a specific project that generates enthusiasm for the salespeople.

Case Study

In Chicago, Molly, a salesperson for a window manufacturer, has been operating as an architectural sales representative for nearly a decade. The manufacturer's dealers in the market eagerly discuss the benefits that Molly provides. Her ability to establish relationships with dozens of architects in the market has given her clout and leverage. The dealers in Chicago consider her the most vital representative to their success, more vital than the local manufacturer's sales representative or regional sales manager. The reason is obvious: Molly is helping the dealers hunt for new business.

The downside for the dealers is that Molly wields control with the local architectural community. She decides how to allocate her leads, which makes the dealers beholden to her. Power resides with the person who controls the quality of the business relationship.

The good news for you is that you can create your own architectural sales program. You don't need to wait for your employer to supply you with a full-time architectural sales representative. Regardless of your job title, you can wield leverage with your customers by establishing vital relationships with architects that influence millions of dollars in business.

6. **Provide account leads, slowly transferring relationship management.** An *account lead* is different from a *project lead*. The project lead is the offer of an immediate sale for your customer. A project lead can evolve into a more general account lead. In fact, this is the desired outcome of any project sale. An account lead is the offer of an ongoing relationship.

Case Study

A manufacturer representative in Detroit, Kevin, worked for a dealer for nearly a decade and had cultivated relationships with many builders in the market. After he took on his new position with a manufacturer, Kevin has remained in business relationships with the many builders in spite of the fact that he rarely generates direct transactions with them. His secret is that he transfers sales responsibility to various dealers in his market. He works directly with his customers' salespeople to manage his relationships with the various builders. On numerous occasions, a customer's salesperson has performed ineffectively, which has required Kevin to intercede and smooth out tense situations. In more than one circumstance, Kevin has resumed control of the relationship with the builder and transferred the sales opportunity to a different salesperson in the marketplace. Kevin's performance provides another example of the power that accompanies the control of the relationship.

---

7. **Sponsor contests to spark interest.** Greg, a Minnesota salesperson for a manufacturer of specialty products, was provided discretionary funds from his employer's marketing department. He decided to use the funds to sponsor a contest with his customers' salespeople. Greg already had strong commitments with these dealers and had established relationships with many of their salespeople. Rather than invest his discretionary marketing funds in traditional ways—e.g., newspaper advertisements, promotional gifts such as hats or golf balls—Greg concluded that he could generate excitement by sponsoring a contest. He would reward his salespeople for performance over a specific period of time. The result was that the salespeople were enthused and became much more comfortable with Greg's products.

Even if you can't sponsor a contest, you might consider ways in which you can challenge individual salespeople and provide other forms of incentive that appeal to them, such as a mention in your company newsletter, a steak dinner, an introduction to an important local leader in the industry, a dozen golf balls with your company logo, and so forth. The key to success is to put a time limit on your incentive program and be prepared to promptly provide the reward your promised.

8. **Keep your salespeople informed.** You may have the support of a media machine behind you, as is the case for billion-dollar companies. But when you work for a smaller organization, you may have to become creative in the ways you keep your customers' salespeople informed. Although your employer and suppliers strive to keep customers and salespeople up-to-date, the information often gets lost in the noisy confusion of the modern world. You can help keep your salespeople current with the creative use of phone calls, e-mails, and personal contact. Salespeople are usually excited by new products, innovations to existing products, and new sales tools. Take advantage of any such changes as a means of creating opportunity for your salespeople.

9. **Use your marketing department effectively.** The communication between marketing and sales is not always ideal. Marketing departments

want to focus on the big picture of branding, campaigns, and trends. Salespeople typically could not care less about these issues, preferring to focus instead on the immediate gratification of a sales opportunity. As a result of the animosity between departments, salespeople often misunderstand and misuse the tools marketing departments create.

You should always consider two important factors when you are selecting effective sales and marketing tools: audience and timing. Take time to review each sales tool to determine for which audience it will be most useful. For example, a piece of product literature that illustrates detailed installation options would be more suitable for an installer or builder than for a consumer. A technical catalog that provides specification details and size charts would be suited to an architect or a builder but probably not a consumer. A piece of literature that provides illustrations and pictures of product applications and design ideas would be ideal for a consumer who is making product selections.

Promotional sales representatives can make all these various tools come to life. Salespeople usually hand out literature with almost no explanation or understanding of the proper use of the tool. Instead, they must take the time to carefully consider the most effective way to use each sales tool in their arsenal. A single piece of literature in the hands of an expert salesperson can be more effective than hundreds of dollars worth of samples in the hands of an amateur. For example, consider a well-designed piece of literature that can help sway a consumer's decision. Sales representatives in promotional sales roles can deftly and calmly describe for builders how they can use that piece of literature to educate their customers.

"Please take a moment," says the expert promotional sales representative, "to look at this wonderful piece of literature. The manufacturer has placed several pictures throughout the brochure that illustrate excellent design ideas using this product. You will be pleased to see that the brochure also shows other products and design concepts that may interest your potential customers. This tool is one that consumers value greatly as a guide during the design- and product-selection process. It provides a fantastic way for you to offer them design ideas while you keep your name in front of them." As the sales representative points to the important blank position on the back of the literature, he or she adds, "On the back of the literature is a handy location for you to put a stamp or a label with your company information and phone number. This is a great way for prospects to remember the design value of your company. If you need a larger supply of these, let me know."

This presentation does more than talk about features and benefits. In fact, the presentation focuses completely on the sales challenges of the reseller, in this case, a builder. Take time to consider the most effective way to use the various sales tools in your arsenal. Then share your ideas with other salespeople to get them enthused and involved with your company and product.

10. Work with inside sales support in the same manner. The implication of most of this book has been that salespeople are usually traveling salespeople, commonly called outside salespeople. There has been no need to delineate between outside and inside salespeople because they do virtually the same thing. Although outside salespeople may be perceived to be more focused on prospecting for new clientele, there is nothing to say that inside salespeople cannot be equally assertive. Inside salespeople manage customer relationships, introduce new products, and educate prospects. They write orders and put out fires. They deal with the stress of angry customers and the joy of closing a sale. In short, inside and outside salespeople perform similar (in many cases, identical) tasks. Inside salespeople can make or break a sales transaction, and, because they are commonly promoted to outside sales positions or management roles, they are key to your future. Thus, skilled promotional sales representatives apply all the strategies and tactics of the previous chapter and this one with both inside and outside salespeople.

The Ultimate Strategy—Sales Leadership

STRATEGY #8:

Become a sales manager.

If you carefully review the tactics from the previous section, you will notice that a trend is emerging, and that the tactics evolve. The tactics represent an evolution from basic sales behaviors into sales management tasks. Behave like a sales manager and you will be respected as a sales management leader, even without the title of "sales manager." The skills of great salespeople allow them to establish a leadership role among their peers, a level of credibility you too can achieve. With the development of these skills, you will earn the right to take on the loftier tasks of sales management. Sales management (all management, for that matter) focuses on two main activities— coaching and supervision.

The tactics of the previous "good" strategy allow you to earn credibility as a *sales coach*. These are tactics that both promotional sales representatives and sales managers should employ. Coaching involves work in the field. Sometimes coaching requires that an individual lead by example, while, at other times, it requires the ability to provide feedback regarding performance. Coaching skills are essential to the credibility of a manager. Many salespeople have worked for managers for whom they have little respect, simply because the managers have never demonstrated the ability to walk in the shoes of those salespeople. A sales manager does not need to be the best salesperson—even the best golfer in the world has a coach. Despite the fact that the coach could not win a tournament, he is still revered for his knowledge. Instead, he earns his coaching credentials through experience, knowledge, trust, and credibility.

Supervision involves management of the sales environment and measurement of performance. Managers who force their salespeople to submit meaningless reports almost always lose their credibility. Managers who create reports that help salespeople make more money gain tremendous credibility. Managers who can help salespeople overcome the suffering of our industry gain even more credibility. Nothing disheartens salespeople more quickly than encountering obstacles to sales success. Obstacles come in a variety of forms. In some cases, a manager can do nothing to alleviate the existence or impact of obstacles except to lend an empathetic ear. In many cases, a manager can help salespeople overcome obstacles and challenges by demonstrating ways for them to concentrate on the big picture. Successful sales management, whether delegated by authority or earned by credibility, ultimately relies on managers' ability to help their salespeople achieve success.

Your ability to manage other salespeople begins long before someone gives you a business card with a new title. The moment you became a salesperson in the construction industry, you were already thrust into a management position of great responsibility. A builder who resells your product relies on your sales-management abilities. A fellow salesperson who needs an empathetic ear relies on your sales-management abilities. You will constantly encounter situations in which your role as a sales manager will be tested and challenged. You will not become a sales manager because someone offers you a promotion. You can only become a sales manager when you develop the skills that allow you to mold yourself into a sales leader who garners the respect of your peers.

10 TACTICS THAT MAKE YOU A SALES MANAGER

1. Know your market.
2. Recruit committed salespeople.
3. Develop a strong database-management method.
4. Create a lead-valuation method.
5. Create a sales purpose for your meetings with customers.
6. Annually review goals with sales leadership and set future new goals.
7. Set sales goals with individual salespeople.
8. Weed out uncommitted salespeople.
9. Don't manage by voice mail and e-mails.
10. Calculate your value and sell it!

Becoming a Sales Manager

The following tactics represent the fundamental skills you must develop to become an effective sales manager:

1. Know your market. In the previous chapter, one tactic suggested that you establish market-share goals. The implication of this tactic is that you know the total potential volume in your market. But volume is only one piece of the puzzle. Skilled salespeople have a deep understanding of the market in which they work. They understand their competitors' products, strengths, weaknesses, and sales volume. They know who the leaders are in the market among all the different disciplines and channels. They are aware of the top builders, remodelers, and architects. They are aware of the top dealers of products by category. The massive amount of information that is available about your market creates a never-ending process of discovery. A skilled sales leader understands that obtaining market knowledge is not a goal to achieve, but rather an eternal process.

2. Recruit committed salespeople. Any sales manager will tell you that sales success relies on the recruitment of a solid sales team. Thus, the most important task of a sales manager is the hiring of the "right" salespeople. Talent and skill are not always the most important criteria by which to evaluate a potential salesperson. A young, mediocre salesperson who is *committed to personal growth* may be preferable to an older, average salesperson who is settled in his or her ways and resistance to instruction. A salesperson who is excited about an opportunity is far superior to one who is merely settling for the first chance that comes along.

As a manufacturer representative, your recruitment (and management) practices will have many similarities to the hiring practices of a sales manager. Just as salespeople focused on personal growth are preferable to those who are resistant to change, average salespeople committed to your product are more valuable that great salespeople who will not offer you their time. You will need to learn what motivates each salesperson in order to help him or her grow and increase your product sales. You will have no opportunity to conduct a formal interview or structure a formal sales offer, but you will have an opportunity to ask questions and learn about the past behaviors and future vision of every sales "candidate." Some salespeople will require significant investments of your time, while others will operate very effectively on their own. Your role with each salesperson, much like that of a skilled sales manager, will vary depending on individual needs.

Although there are many similarities, there is one glaring difference between your role and that of a sales manager. Obviously, you will not have the same degree of delegated authority over the salespeople you recruit. You will be forced to rely upon the credibility you establish with your sales team. Credibility places you in a realm in which salespeople are attracted to your strength and welcome the chance to work with you. Develop your credibility, and then you can recruit a sales team who participate enthusiastically in the programs you offer. Salespeople will recognize that your sales leadership can help them sell more of *all* their products as they work with you to sell more of *your* products.

3. Develop a strong database-management method. This area is one in which salespeople's behaviors often dramatically fall short of their values. Every salesperson recognizes the importance of managing a database of contacts. But most salespeople somehow fall short of putting this management system into practice. Database-management skills relieve the suffering caused by confusing distribution channels. An expert salesperson recognizes that every contact represents potential growth in sales, power, and credibility. The expert puts a structured program in place to manage the contact information in a way that simplifies the confusion of distribution channels. The database lets salespeople retain personal information as well as business data on their customers. Many salespeople recognize the value of knowing customers' birthdates and hobbies. And although this personal information is valuable, much more important is that they note business information—sales volume, competing products, business strengths, and so forth.

The first key to successful database management is to recognize that your system must accommodate constant changes and updates. Thus, a paper method, while acceptable, is inferior to the excellent software programs that are available today. Paper database systems get messy and time consuming. Salespeople who keep stacks of business cards bound by rubber bands are cheating themselves of valuable opportunities left untapped. Computer software programs let you put much more detail into your records, and they facilitate data retrieval and sorting. Computer software programs provide the opportunity to quickly add and edit important information about prospects and customers.

The second key to successful database-management methods is to commit to using only *one* database. This commitment may require you to include personal contacts with business contacts. It certainly requires you to include contact information regarding prospects and customers in one single database. If you have divided your territory into manageable zones, you will discover that your productivity is dramatically improved when you have your prospects and customers grouped together. Thus, you can maximize the value of your time by meeting with prospects in between customer visits and avoid lengthy travel.

The singular database also reminds you to evaluate opportunities equally. For example, if measured in terms of total sales, one of your customer's salespeople might be more valuable than an entire dealer's business. And so you would recognize that managing the individual relationships is often more important than managing your overall business relationships with a dealer. People are the key to success.

The volume of sales the resellers of your product achieve determines promotional sales success. Database-management skills help promotional sales representatives evaluate and manage relationships. Promotional sales representatives should share their database-management methods with salespeople, to help them grow in their careers.

4. **Create a lead-valuation method.** A database lets you manage many different pieces of information about customers and prospects. A *lead-valuation method* is different in that it should be designed solely to measure the value of sales opportunities and monitor their progress. A *lead* is any sales opportunity that can be quantified. Database information includes names, addresses, phone numbers, and the like. A lead can be a project, a proposed development, a new prospect, a salesperson, or any other sales opportunity for which a value can be given. The next chapter offers insights into specific methods of lead valuation. The purpose of the lead valuation is to provide confidence toward achieving your goals. An essential byproduct of your lead valuation is the ability to help other salespeople manage their goals.

5. **Create a sales purpose for your meetings with customers.** If you have taken the time to quantify your activity (from the previous tactic), you will have ample information about sales opportunities in the market. You will know the value of opportunities, where they lie, and at what stage of the process they are. Thus, when you meet with your customers, you can avoid the common pitfall of average salespeople who are focused excessively on service (i.e., farming) activities. Average salespeople, who frequently confuse activity and productivity, lack strong reasons for their meetings with customers. If salespeople have no purpose when they meet resellers of their products, then they should expect the customers to request extensive service support. The customers will ask the salespeople to price products, check on orders, handle after-sale service issues, and the like. But these activities are not where skilled promotional sales representatives should invest the majority of their time. They should invest their time in the field with their customers' customers and salespeople.

When skilled promotional sales representatives do meet with customers, the purpose of those meetings is to discuss sales opportunities. Expert salespeople can focus the meetings on issues related to sales growth. Therefore, skilled promotional sales representatives meet with customers to discuss the leads they have produced, marketing programs, training programs, and the joint sales efforts they have developed for their customers.

6. **Annually review goals with sales leadership and set future goals.** One of the most challenging discussions manufacturer representatives have with customers is the discussion of sales goals. Manufacturers frequently behave paternalistically, assuming that they have the right to dictate sales goals to dealers. The manufacturer tries to apply pressure to the dealer by threatening to expand the network of dealers in the market. The dealer responds by acquiring additional product lines, and a combative relationship ensues.

Manufacturer representatives are in a position to relieve the pressure by earning the right to have the discussion of sales goals and quotas. They can produce sales opportunities that create leverage as well as enthusiasm! If promotional sales representatives produce sales, then they have earned the right to discuss annual goals. Dealers are happy to commit to realistic sales goals when they believe they have a cooperative relationship. Your ability to set goals that customers accept is contingent upon your ability to generate sales opportunities in the market.

7. **Set sales goals with individual salespeople.** You can also take time, as a promotional sales representative, to create sales goals with individual salespeople. The individual sales goals of salespeople should be consistent with the goal you have for their entire organization. If you have a customer with five salespeople and a goal of $500,000, you know that each salesperson should average $100,000. If the salespeople are not aware of the goals you have established, you might discover their expectations differ vastly from yours. Take time to meet with individual salespeople periodically to discuss their sales-volume goals for your product.

Your success with this strategy is contingent, once again, upon your ability to generate sales and leads for your salespeople. If you have nothing to offer, you should expect nothing in return. If you have successfully fulfilled all the previous tactics, you have earned the right to expect some form of accountability in return. After all, you are putting bread on their table when you provide them with sales leads.

8. **Weed out uncommitted salespeople.** It will happen that, even when you are supplying valuable leads to salespeople, some of them simply will not embrace your efforts. That does not mean they are unable to contribute to your success. It simply means that you need to be careful how much of your resources you devote to their cause. If you provide training, leads, sales support, and other resources to a customer's salespeople, only to discover that those individuals choose to ignore the benefits, then simply find other salespeople with whom you can share the wealth. Just as you periodically lose customers, you will also lose salespeople. Roll with the punches, and you will discover that your success grows. The salespeople who value your contributions will become increasingly loyal. After you weed them out, the salespeople who resist your contributions may later come to realize they should take your leadership role more seriously.

Case Study

When I was an architectural sales representative, I continually provided sales leads to a small network of dealers. I specifically gave leads to individual salespeople so I could better create accountability in the process. One salesperson, Bob, had received four different leads from me over the course of a few weeks. He expressed enthusiastic gratitude for the sales opportunities. I asked numerous times for feedback on the progress of the sales opportunities, but

Bob persistently shrugged me off, citing his busy schedule. Because Bob was a successful salesperson at his dealership and a solid producer of sales for my company, I was between a rock and hard place. If I pushed him to acquiesce to my requests for feedback, I ran the risk of irritating a successful contributor to my organization. If I ignored the situation, I would not achieve my sales objectives. I did the only thing possible by silently "firing" Bob by giving him no further leads.

I was stunned when Bob invited me to his private golf club a few months later. During the day, he was pleasant and accommodating. His generosity was flattering. At one of the last holes on the course, Bob cautiously asked me why he wasn't getting any more leads. I smiled cordially and told him that he didn't need to invite me golfing to get leads. He merely needed to keep me updated on the progress of the leads I had given him, and hopefully sell some of them. The conversation was brief and to the point. From that day forward, Bob happily gave me brief updates on the leads that I supplied, and I continued to put bread on his table in the form of great leads.

Had Bob not come to me with a request to be reinstated into my "program," I would have simply continued to operate without his assistance and weeded him out of the program. Promotional sales representatives do not have the luxury of "firing" employees, but they can replace uncommitted salespeople with enthusiastic participants.

---

9. **Don't manage by voice mail and e-mails.** The technical revolution has created wonderful opportunities for efficiency and enhanced communication. The downside of the technical revolution is that the technologies are often misused. Managers and salespeople frequently abuse the convenience of voice mail and e-mail. The problem with these mediums is that they do not permit open dialogue. Every day, human beings throughout the country send e-mails laced with criticism and negative information to employees, coworkers, and customers. Recipients have no ability to respond to the negativity except with defensive e-mails and voice mails in return. A popular tactic among department and organization leaders is to send out mass e-mails and voice mails with directives and imperatives. The leaders don't realize that they are probably creating resentment around the water cooler with no improvement to productivity for the recipients of the message.

If you have bad news to deliver, make a point to deliver the information directly to the recipient. Schedule a face-to-face meeting or a phone call that will allow the recipient to deal with the situation fairly. Direct communication is the best way to effectively change behavior. If you deliver negative information in an e-mail or voice mail, chances are that you will create only animosity in the human being on the receiving end.

10. **Calculate your value and sell it!** Some of the best salespeople in our business have contributed immensely to their organizations and to other people. Salespeople who sponsor training seminars for their customers help them become more successful selling not only the sponsor's products, but every product in the salespeoples' arsenal. A lead that helps salespeople sell even one product to a builder might be the catalyst that launches a long-term relationship that allows those salespeople to sell the same builder multiple products over many years.

A dealer who was reluctant to purchase displays in accordance with the manufacturer's requirements told the manufacturer's representative that he would use the displays if the manufacturer provided them for free. The salesperson responded that the displays were not free and were a symbol of commitment to the program. The dealer was adamant in his position. Then the salesperson reminded the dealer that he had provided more than one-half million dollars in business to the dealer the previous year. He calmly offered the dealer a choice between purchasing the displays or forfeiting the next $500,000 in the manufacturer representative's sales. As you might expect, the dealer was sold on the manufacturer representative's value and acquiesced to the program requirement.

The value you bring to your customers extends well beyond the products you sell, or least it should. Skilled salespeople create value for their customers with sales, ideas, communication, networking opportunities, knowledge, training, and more. Your leadership will grow as you become more credible in your sales skills. And as you continue to develop your sales skills, seek ways to share your knowledge and energy for the benefit of others. Your value will grow, and you will achieve the greatest goal—happiness.

CHAPTER EIGHT

MEASURING
SALES SUCCESS

I n the practice of science, the only way to duplicate the results of an experiment is to carefully measure the data. If you want to vary the results, then you must change the input. Whether you are duplicating or varying the results, you will never fully control the outcome if you have not measured the data. We can apply the same methods that work in scientific study to business in general, and to the profession of selling in particular. In fact, we can assert that an invariable law of selling is that we cannot improve performance if we cannot measure it.

Although it is true that many salespeople are successful even without adopting any procedures to measure their performance, a crisis eventually arises when those individuals find themselves falling far short of their expected performance goals. The typical sales-management methods within the construction industry focus mainly on the measurement of sales volume. If sales volume is high, salespeople are doing well; if sales volume is low, salespeople are doing poorly.[1]

---

[1] Sales volume alone may not be the best measure of performance because it is not even the final goal of an organization. Profit is the ultimate objective. In recent years, many manufacturers and distributors of materials have implemented compensation structures that align with their salespeople and the objectives of the organization. These compensation structures specifically reward salespeople for generating profit-margin dollars, in lieu of sales volume incentives. For simplicity, the lessons of this chapter focus on examples related to sales volume only. The lessons are easily convertible for use when gross margin is the measure of performance.

Case Studies

The value of the showroom. In New Hampshire, Scott noticed that, when customers visited his showroom, his success was immense. He conducted no formal study but concluded, "at least 75 percent of the people who visited [his] showroom prior to receiving a price became customers." What he needed to do was obvious. He made it his primary objective to invite every one of his potential customers to his showroom, to create the strongest opportunity to make the sale. The success of his sales effort was based upon his observation of a critical statistic.

Margin involvement. At a large lumberyard chain in the Midwest, the sales manager restructured compensation to reward salespeople for generating higher sales margins. The structure of the program was relatively complex, creating differing margin incentives to improve the sales of weaker products. The results were immediate. As sales margins rose, the impact to the bottom line was evident instantly. The profit to the company rose from 1 percent to 3 percent the year following the adjustment, while sales of flagging products also rose. Analysis of objective data pointed up the need for the margin-incentive program, and the sales manager used simple analytical tools to evaluate the program's success. Creating measurement tools is not difficult when you know what to look for.

The value of self-measurement. After attending one of our seminars, Matt, a salesperson for a manufacturer of specialty building materials, began to list every new lead he discovered. His list included company names, contact information, and the potential value of every sale. Within only a few weeks, Matt discovered that he would need to generate more leads if he was going to have a legitimate opportunity to achieve his annual sales goal. Matt eventually became one of the few salespeople among a staff of 20 who expressed confidence that he would achieve his annual sales goal. He has since emerged as a leader in his organization. While many of his peers talk fearfully about their

10 TACTICS THAT HELP YOU QUANTIFY PERFORMANCE

1. Measure your sales volume.
2. Quantify your meeting activity.
3. Calculate your appointment value.
4. Evaluate the quality of your appointment activity.
5. Count and rate your prospects and customers.
6. Measure your prospecting activity.
7. Measure your closing ratios.
8. Determine your rate of attrition.
9. Know the 100 percent guaranteed method to achieve your sales goals.
10. Eat an elephant one bite at a time.

(past) sales volume, Matt is always focused and excited about the opportunities ahead.

STRATEGY # 9:

Quantify your performance to
improve performance.

Quantifying Performance

To quantify your performance, develop your skills with the following 10 tactics:

1. Measure your sales volume. You probably are asking yourself why someone would tell you to measure your sales volume. Even the most mediocre salespeople know the importance of this statistic. Yet the employer typically initiates the measurement of sales volume while salespeople wait passively for the information. Every month, their employer provides a statement that tells them how much they sold. That report usually provides additional information, such as sales during the month, year-to-date sales, and a comparison of prior year sales for the same period. So why would salespeople need to do more?

Howard, a salesman for a manufacturer of wood windows, habitually filed and tallied the copies of his customers' invoices that his employer supplied. He tracked the purchasing activity of each account and personally entered the data into a journal. At the conclusion of each month, he and his manager played a game to see how similar their numbers were. They were never exactly the same because of adjustments to invoices, payment discounts, and other factors that Howard was unable to count. However, their numbers were close enough that Howard's sales manager considered him to be the most organized salesperson he had ever met. Howard figured that it took him approximately one hour per week to enter the data. His efforts created in him a deep awareness of the trends in his territory and with his customers. His proactive pursuit and observation of this simple information distinguished him from his competitors and strengthened his credibility with customers.

Most salespeople merely wait for whatever information their employer will offer. They look at the data and focus on the sales volume, rarely taking time to analyze all the insightful ways that the data identify improvement opportunities.

For example, you can break down your sales volume by customer. You can further categorize the data by classifying customers as existing and new; you might naturally expect long-term, existing customers to be relatively stable or growing, while new customers will hopefully be on a rapid rise. If you have set sales goals with your customers, you can track their individual performance to discover where you are meeting account goals and where you are falling short. You will probably discover trends in the data that you never expected. You might envision many other ways in which observation of the data can help you. The only certainty is that you will learn very little about the data if you do not track it carefully.

Spreadsheet technology provides an excellent method by which you can measure the overall performance of your sales career. You can also use spreadsheets to measure the performance of each account that makes up the total of your sales volume. (See "Appendix A—Customer Tracking" for a spreadsheet template that helps evaluate both account performance and overall sales trends.) The use of spreadsheets and computer databases is becoming so prevalent that why some salespeople do not use these options extensively in their self-management efforts defies logic. In a world of acute competition and advanced technology, using pencil and paper to track data is like going to war with a musket.

2. Quantify your meeting activity. Woody Allen said, "Ninety percent of life is just showing up." Likewise, one of the simplest ways to measure sales performance is to count the number of meetings you average per week. This simple measurement is often salespeople's most important determiner of success. Even mediocre salespeople will succeed if they simply show up enough. It is commonly said that selling is a "percentage game," which is true. The unfortunate (or fortunate, depending where your percentages fall) reality is that some salespeople have better percentages than others. The measure of salespeople's *skill* is in the percentages. Similarly, the measure of salespeople's *desire* can be evaluated by the level of activity they create. And the best measurement of salespeople's activity is their number of meetings with customers and prospects.

For the purposes of objective measurement, consider every face-to-face business encounter a "meeting." If you visit with an important customer for an entire day to plan out the future of your relationship, then that is one meeting. If you drop off a piece of literature to a potential new customer (*not* the receptionist), then that is one meeting, even if the meeting lasts less than five minutes. If you meet a customer at a jobsite to inspect a product defect, that is a meeting. A physical cold call to an office is a meeting. For the sake of this exercise, any belly-to-belly encounter counts as one meeting.

The number of weekly meetings salespeople have will vary depending on the product, region, and segment of the industry in which they sell. Some salespeople typically make 25 to 40 sales calls per week, while others fill a complete schedule with 15 meetings. More often than not, salespeople are *not* making as many sales calls as they possibly can. They fail to plan their time adequately, or they lack incentive. Salespeople frequently ask during our training seminars how many meetings they "should" have in a typical day or week. No one can answer that question except to say that there is no such thing as a "typical day." With that caveat in mind, it is fair to say that dealer salespeople generally should have more meetings than manufacturer sales representatives. It is also fair to say that the level of activity for any sales representative will vary based on any number of factors—e.g., inside sales support, customer types, product issues, and the geography of one's territory. There is no absolute definition of what a salesperson's activity level "should" be, except to say we can draw the two following conclusions:

- Most salespeople do not know how many meetings they make on average per week.
- Most salespeople can have *more* meetings.

The purpose of counting your activity is to reveal the possibilities that exist. When you discover that you can make one more appointment every day, sometimes two if you plan your time wisely, then you will quickly discover that doing this is the easiest way to increase your sales volume. You will discover that the more meetings you have, the more success you achieve.

3. Calculate your appointment value. The first tactic of this section tells you to calculate your sales volume, and the second tactic tells you to count the number of weekly meetings you conduct. Those two simple approaches allow you to calculate the average value of your sales meetings. When you take time to measure the value of time, you discover a simple method to improve your performance and achieve better results.

To calculate meeting value, divide the number of meetings you make per year by your total sales volume during the year. To estimate how many meetings you make per year (assuming you haven't taken the time to really count your total meetings during the preceding 12 months), multiply the number of weekly meetings by 50. Let us say a salesperson is averaging 24 sales calls (meetings) per week, while generating $1,000,000 in annual sales. A salesperson who makes 24 sales calls per week for 50 weeks per year makes 1,200 sales calls annually. If that were the case, the salesperson would quickly be able to calculate that each meeting was therefore worth $833.

Annual Sales Volume/Number of Meetings = Meeting Value
Example: $1,000,000/1200 = $833

The only reason to evaluate the historic worth of your meetings is to plan future activity. If you want to improve your performance, you measure your past performance, and then make adjustments for the future. Equipped with their *meeting value,* salespeople can now plan their future sales volume. Salespeople who do the same thing they have always done will get the same result. The reverse of the formula is also true. Therefore salespeople who do the same thing will get the game result.

$$\text{Meeting Value} \times \text{Number of Meetings} = \text{Annual Sales Volume}$$
$$\text{Example: } \$833 \times 1,200 = \$1,000,000$$

Salespeople who change what they have always done will get different results. You can plan to increase your sales volume in either or both of two ways:

1. You can make more sales calls.
2. You can increase your value per sales call.

The strategies and tactics outlined in earlier chapters were created to help you increase the value of your sales effort per sales call, but there is no substitute for hard work. The simplest way to increase your sales totals is to make more meetings. Thus, the next time you are ready to call it a day, make one more sales call. If you're in an office building to visit an architect, look at the building directory to see whether there is another architect in the same building. If you have an hour between meetings, look in your portable database for a new prospect. Stop by every jobsite if you have extra time on your drive to your next meeting. If you run out of prospects by the middle of the afternoon, find the yellow pages. Find any means by which you can meet an additional prospect or customer every day, and then two additional prospects per day. The short-term benefit may feel negligible, but the long-term benefit of the extra sales effort becomes quantifiable and meaningful.

Let's assume that a salesperson is on the street *four days per week*. It is fair to figure that, on average, this salesperson will need to divert approximately 20 percent of the time away from sales and promotional efforts for various activities such as seminars, emergencies, office days, and the like. Thus, if this salesperson makes one extra sales call on four of the five days per week which means an additional 200 sales calls by the end of the year.

The extra sales call that felt negligible during a last-minute stop in the afternoon suddenly takes on significant proportions by the end of the year. The salesperson selling $833 per sales call and making 200 extra sales calls per year would increase annual sales by $166,600!

$$200 \times \$833 = \$166,600$$

If salespeople can improve the value of each meeting, their success will be even greater. For example, if you as our sample salesperson improved your performance to $1,000 per sales call, you would sell an additional $200,000 (1,200 × $1,000 = $1,200,000) per year *without* any additional sales meetings. If you were to make an additional sales call every day *and* increase your meeting value, you would sell an additional $400,000 (1,400 × $1,000 = $1,400,000) per year, a 40 percent increase! And one way in which you can easily improve the value of each meeting is to improve the *quality of the meeting structure*.

4. Evaluate the quality of your appointment activity. Most salespeople in the construction industry make three types of sales calls: appointments, cold calls, and something we will call a warm call. An *appointment* is simply what one would consider a traditional meeting that has been scheduled for a specific date and time and, hopefully, with a planned purpose. A *cold call* is a meeting or phone call to a prospect who has no expectation of the visit. The term *warm call* might be new to many salespeople. A *warm call* is a meeting with a customer who at least has the expectation of a meeting, although no time for the meeting has been specifically scheduled. Without being entirely specific about a time or possibly even a date, a salesperson might simply ask a prospect or customer whether it would be acceptable for the salesperson stop in for a brief meeting. The purpose of scheduling a warm call is to avoid being denied an appointment altogether. Many people don't like to commit to meetings far in advance, but they are willing to meet if you "catch" them in their office. A warm call satisfies these conditions and reduces the tension that often accompanies a cold call.

The most common methods for scheduling appointments are phone calls. The term we commonly give to an unsolicited phone call to a prospect is a *cold call.* For the purposes of this quantification exercise, I would like to expand the concept of a cold call to include even a physical meeting. The normal purpose of a cold call conducted by phone is to solicit an appointment. Therefore, the purpose for a physical, in-person cold call should be no different. For some reason, however, salespeople commonly make physical cold calls to offices or jobsites during their daily travels and expect prospects to be excited about a lengthy dialogue with an intrusive salesperson. The purpose of any cold call should merely be to schedule a future appointment. If the physical cold call results in an immediate meeting (i.e., the prospect invites the salesperson to continue), all the better. An expert salesperson recognizes that the purpose of a cold call is to schedule a future meeting, and nothing more.

The three types of sales calls generally result in different levels of productivity. A scheduled appointment is a meeting that produces the greatest likelihood for productivity. A warm call will produce likelihood for some productivity, while a cold call should be expected to yield only modest results. Some salespeople might dispute this hierarchy, asserting that any call might result in a tremendous sales opportunity. This is of course true, but when one honestly appraises the *likelihood* of such results (based on percentages of success), most industry professionals would agree that salespeople will probably have more success when they have scheduled appointments with customers.

During a coaching session I held with a brand new salesperson for a manufacturer of millwork materials, he noted, while on our way to a meeting, that we had no appointment, but he felt assured that the customer was "always in his office and would not be difficult to see." This was a bold assumption, considering that we were driving more than half an hour to the destination. When we arrived at the office, the purchasing agent for the lumberyard stated, "I'd love to meet with you guys! In fact, I was wondering when someone from your company would call on me. Unfortunately, I am quite busy today. Call me next week to make an appointment." We had wasted an hour of our day to accomplish what could have been done with a simple phone call. Nor did this salesperson get off to a very credible start with the potential customer. This cold call was an expensive investment in time, and it demonstrates the obvious. The value of an appointment is greater than the value of a warm call, both of which are infinitely greater than the value of a cold call.

Figure 8.1 depicts a week that is very common among unproductive salespeople. Each line in the figure represents a meeting. The solid line represents a scheduled appointment; the dashed line represents a warm call; the dotted line represents a cold call. The figure represents a salesperson who had only three appointments per week and filled in the time with cold calls. Notice that the salesperson was inconsistent with his or her activity, and one might expect the salesperson's performance from week to week also to be inconsistent. Notice that the salesperson made only 17 sales calls for the entire week, far below potential.

Figure 8.2 illustrates a week that indicates better planning and efficiency. The salesperson has obviously invested time scheduling appointments and warm calls. The salesperson has also filled in the week by making cold calls, keeping activity levels high. Notice that the weekly activity level for this salesperson is higher despite the fact that no sales calls were made on Thursday. This salesperson needed Thursday as an office day to handle administrative tasks and to invest time on the phone scheduling appointments for the upcoming week. Notice that this salesperson took advantage of prime selling time on Friday afternoon, the time when customers and prospects are often the happiest, and most competitors have already given

FIGURE 8.1 Inexperienced/Inefficient Salesperson

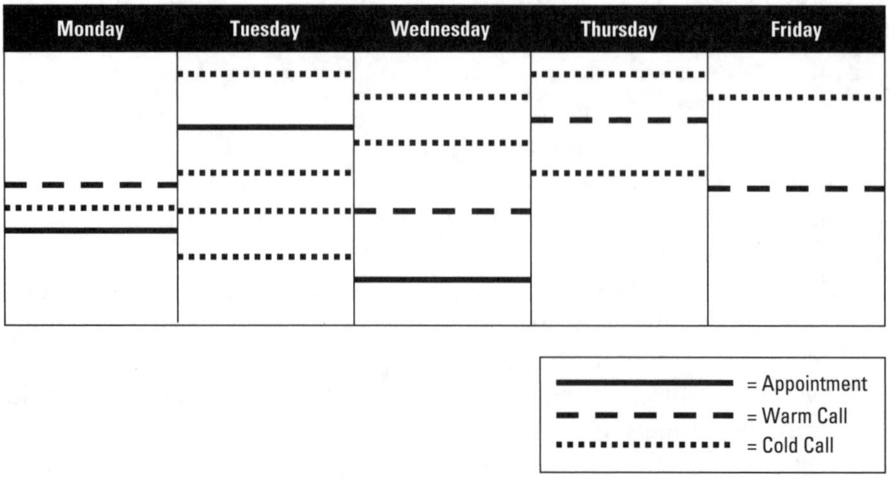

Monday	Tuesday	Wednesday	Thursday	Friday

————— = Appointment
— — — — — = Warm Call
················· = Cold Call

FIGURE 8.2 Growing Salesperson

Monday	Tuesday	Wednesday	Thursday	Friday

                                                    ————— = Appointment
                                                    — — — — = Warm Call
                                                    ·············· = Cold Call

up for the week. This salesperson achieved his or her personal goal of 30 sales calls for the week late on Friday afternoon.

There is no reason to assume that all appointments are scheduled by phone. In fact, it would be difficult to schedule every appointment by making a phone call. Builders are often difficult to reach by phone, which indicates that some appointments should be scheduled during physical visits. At the conclusion of each meeting, whenever appropriate, salespeople should schedule the next appointment. All too often, salespeople conclude meetings with the idea that they can later call and easily schedule a follow-up appointment, never considering that they can schedule the appointment while they have the person right in front of them.

Figure 8.3 illustrates the activity of the best salespeople in our industry. They continually are busy and often schedule their time two or three weeks ahead, rarely reacting to customer demands that would create major disruptions to their schedule. Despite the quality of the activity, our star performer always finds time to make cold calls and meet new prospects. There are certainly situations in which emergencies occur, and salespeople must accept deviations to their schedules. The difference between mediocre performers and the best salespeople in the industry is often most apparent in the quality of their schedules and their calendar management. Notice that Wednesday morning and Thursday afternoon were administrative days for the accomplished salesperson in Figure 8.3. You may notice that our accomplished performer had 33 calls that week, although salespeople like this may be unaware of such a fact because they have advanced their careers to a point at which they are measuring other performance data. If you ever have the opportunity to observe the performance of accomplished salespeople, you will discover that their activity is intense and effortless. They always

FIGURE 8.3 Accomplished Salesperson

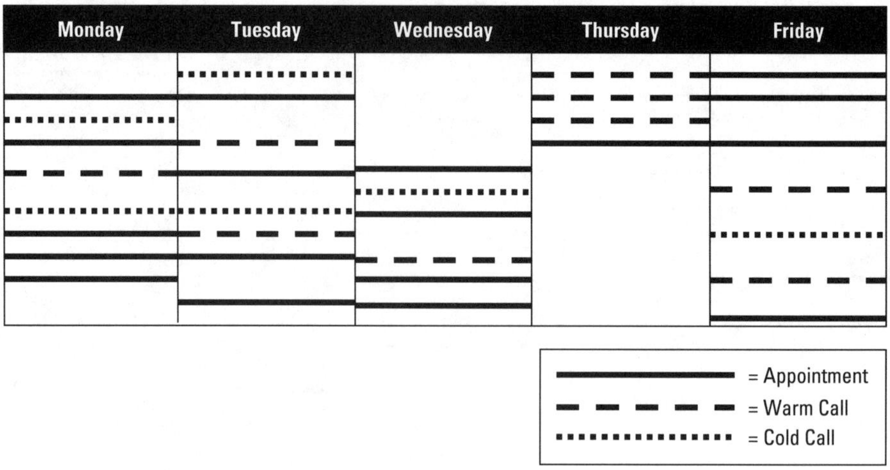

manage another sales call. Customers are "expecting" them. They are continually scheduling meetings one and two weeks in advance.

Although Figure 8.1 represents the activity one would *expect* of a salesperson at the start of his or her career that is being overly assumptive. There is no reason to assume that the salespeople in Figure 8.2 or Figure 8.3 have more years of experience than the salesperson in Figure 8.1. Many sales veterans would be surprised to discover that they have duplicated their first year of experience repeatedly for decades and still have activity levels similar to that portrayed in Figure 8.1. Alternatively, some salespeople achieve the productivity depicted in Figure 8.2 within a few months of their career start. For that reason, the labels on the three figures are not intended to represent "experience," but rather to correspond to proficiency and attitude. An old saying asserts, "There is no substitute for experience." While this wise adage is true, it also understates the importance of growth and the pursuit of excellence. Experience is no guarantee of success. You can repeat one year of experience 20 times, or you can experience 20 years of growth.

> You can repeat one year of experience 20 times, or you can experience 20 years of growth.

In this section, we scrutinized only one aspect of sales activity. You also can evaluate your activity to ensure that your time is properly balanced between existing customers (farming) and prospecting for new customers (hunting). You can further evaluate how well you are investing your time by counting the meetings you have with grade A and grade B accounts versus less profitable opportunities. If you are a manufacturer representative striving to create pull-through sales opportunities, you might count your number of builder and architect calls relative to your number of dealer calls. There are multitudes of ways in which you can evaluate the *quality of your activity*. You should use the ones that are most effective for you.

5. Count and rate your prospects and customers. Your effort to count and rate the entries in your database (i.e., your list of customers and prospects) will help you recognize valuable time-management opportunities. For instance, if you have 30 customers and 10 prospects in your database, you should instinctively recognize the need to evaluate the quality and quantity of your prospect list. When you realize that even if you make continuous contact with the 10 prospects, and you have an excellent 30 percent closing ratio, you would still add only 3 new customers from this "hit list." If you are in this position, you clearly need to increase your number of prospects.

Instead, let's say that you have more than 100 active customers. You might discover that you spend significant time trying to manage the service (i.e., farming) demands of this large customer base, which leaves little time for prospecting. If your customer base is providing you with satisfactory sales results, there is no problem. But if you are not achieving your sales objectives, you would benefit by rating your customers to help prioritize your time. For example, if you discovered that you were allocating the exact same time to Grade A customers and Grade C customers, you would quickly discover that you can improve your time management by devoting more time to your profitable customers. It is not unusual for salespeople to discover that they are devoting more time to secondary customers merely because they are more sociable or geographically convenient. Rate your customers to make proper business decisions regarding the allocation of your time.

Or let's say you are starting out in a new position. You might discover that you have more than 200 prospects and a very small number of active customers. You might find that you are involved in excessive bid-and-pray tactics that are reducing your opportunities to develop strong business relationships. You would benefit by rating your *prospect* determine ways to prioritize your time with the best prospects.

The organization of your database should include both quantitative and qualitative examinations. Rate your customers and prospects to help create a qualitative examination that lets you prioritize your activity. The formulas in Chapter 3 were created to help you evaluate the potential value of customers and prospects. In Chapter 5, the ABCs of rating customers provided a simplistic method to help you manage large amounts of information. Your database should include a field in which you specifically designate a rating for every customer and prospect. Whether you choose to make your database simple or complex, ratings are an essential component of database management. Without a method to rate the *potential* value of every prospect and customer, they all appear equal. The ratings may matter little in your initial development of contacts. But by the time you have developed a list of more than 200 names, you will have no other way to memorize the value of each contact.

Your instincts in this process are more valuable than you may believe. At the conclusion of every meeting with a prospect, ask yourself the benchmark question: "How much should I be visiting this prospect (or customer)?" Your answer will tell you all you need to know to create an amazingly satisfying rating system. If your answer is "All the time; this feels like a great opportunity," then the customer rating is an A. If your answer is "This customer has potential; maybe a lot," then the customer rating is a B. If your answer is "This prospect has value but will probably need my services only periodically," or "I can service this account over the phone and with occasional visits," then the customer rating is a C. The problem for many salespeople is that they spend too much time with Cs. It is better to drive past a C account to solicit a better opportunity.

Keep in mind that all ratings are relative. For instance, an architect who specializes in the design of upscale theaters and opera houses would be an ideal prospect for a salesperson of commercial carpeting or designer fabrics. The same architect would be of little value to a kitchen cabinet salesperson.

And always remember that the process is continuous. A remodeler who is constructing only a few patio additions today might evolve into an organization that specializes in major residential renovations within a few years. An architect who seemed to have potential might display so much loyalty to a competitor that you later choose to downgrade that architect as a result of your observation. More power to you in such cases, because you should confidently and persistently rate your database in a way that works for you!

6. **Measure your prospecting activity.** In the previous chapter, one tactic recommended that you create a lead-valuation system. As a sales expert, you will be truly serious about measuring your performance, and you will recognize that tracking leads is an essential component to sales success. The suffering of win-lose thinking will be alleviated by accepting that you will not sell every prospect. Your success will be a function of your prospecting activity multiplied by your closing ratio. You will virtually eliminate the suffering of win-lose thinking by developing a system that creates a comprehensive method by which you can monitor the value, progress, and outcome of your sales leads. The spreadsheet template in "Appendix A—Customer Tracking" will help you measure your prospecting performance.

The benefit of the spreadsheet will grow as you use it diligently. If you commit to a program in which you enter new sales opportunities daily, you will discover important trends that help you manage your performance. The capability to sort data lets you track activities by customer, follow-up dates, results, and more. As you develop your spreadsheet information, you will be able to measure your closing ratios and your weekly, monthly, and annual activity. At the conclusion of the year, you can roll over all projects and sales opportunities that are still open into the upcoming year, which will give you a head start on your new goals.

7. **Measure your closing ratios.** Notice that this tactic suggests that you measure your closing ratios, plural. You can measure a variety of closing ratios. For instance, if you have 30 prospects, and you acquire three new customers from that list of 30, your ratio of *prospect closing* is 10 percent. Another ratio that we might arbitrarily call your ratio of *customer bid closing*

measures your success rate with existing customers. You should expect that you will close a majority of bids with existing customers, perhaps more than 90 percent. A third closing ratio, the most important, is the one that measures your percentage of sales volume quoted with new customers. For example, a salesperson who bids $2,000,000 and closes $240,000 with prospects who are not active customers would have a closing ratio of 12 percent. This last ratio might be named the *prospect bid closing.* If you are serious about measuring your success as a hunter, you will focus on this last closing ratio as your measure of proficiency. Spreadsheets provide the modern tool that lets you manipulate massive amounts of data in a matter of seconds.

As a final example, consider the Prospect Closing #2 ratio at the bottom of Figure 8.4. This value illustrates both the challenge of measuring, and the accuracy with which one can measure, past performance. Assume that every prospect in this example were worth $30,000. Thus, the total sales opportunity would be $900,000 (30 × $30,000). In the real world, signing up customers takes time. If you were the salesperson in this example and were truly diligent, you would discover that you had signed up three new customers at different times of the year: one after three months, another after six months, and a third after nine months. You could glean many useful pieces of information from these data, most significantly that your closing ratio in real dollars is actually 5 percent, not the 10 percent you calculated using the previous prospect-closing ratio. In other words, you gained only $45,000 of the potential sales volume. As you use the spreadsheets to track sales, you will discover your actual closing ratios. The actual percentages will provide remarkably useful data to help you in your future planning.

8. **Determine your rate of attrition.** *Attrition* is the erosion of your customer base that occurs as a result of lost customers, or decreasing purchases from retained accounts. Most salespeople can offset their attrition rate by inflation (i.e., price increases) and by growing purchases from newer customers. Various studies have shown that the attrition rate of businesses varies between 10 percent and 15 percent annually. However, your customers'

FIGURE 8.4 Closing Ratios

Closing Ratio Category	Potential	Closed	Ratio
Prospect Closing #1	30 Prospects	3 New Customers	10%
Customer Bids	$ 400,000	$ 360,000	90%
Prospect Bids	$ 2,000,000	$ 240,000	12%
Prospect Closing #2	$ 900,000	$ 45,000	5%

This chart gives you examples of various closing ratios that you may consider worth tracking. You would expect that bids to existing customers are likely to result in sales. Thus the closing ratio for customer bids is very high. On the other hand, your closing ratio with new projects may be much lower. The prospect closing #2 deviates from prospect closing #1 in that the former measures the number of customers while the latter measures the value of the potential.

attrition rate is unique to you, and it can be calculated. Once again, the spreadsheet in "Appendix A—Customer Tracking" lets you track your customer activity and evaluate your personal rate of attrition. Your ability to measure your rate of attrition will help you to establish future goals. Over the course of a year, you are going to lose some of your business. This loss is natural and the result of a variety of factors that include customer dissatisfaction, economic downturns, changing needs, and so forth. Your proficiency at evaluating your attrition rate will have an impact on your ability to successfully achieve your sales goals.

9. **Know the 100 percent guaranteed method to achieve your sales goals.** At this point, you have enough data to guarantee yourself a systematic method for achieving lofty sales goals. You must recognize that your ability to make this guarantee is contingent upon your ability to accurately measure your historical performance. When you have successfully completed the previous eight tactics, you will be comfortably prepared to achieve your highest sales goals.

The first step in goal setting is to set a target for your *overall sales increase goal,* the sales volume over your previous end-of-year totals. Most people end their goal-setting process with this step, hoping that they will achieve the goal and conceding, "Sometimes things work out, and sometimes they don't." Unfortunately, this isn't a very satisfying way to find happiness in a sales career. After you have set your overall sales goal, the rest of the goal-setting process is a simple matter of deduction. The next step is to create a *net sales increase goal.* This goal includes consideration for both attrition and growth from your existing customer base. If you expect that growth from your existing customer base will be greater than the attrition rate, then your net sales increase goal will be *less* than your overall sales increase goal (i.e., existing customers will account for some of the overall sales growth). If the attrition rate is greater than the sales growth from existing customers, then your net sales goal will be *greater* than your overall sales goal. The *net sales increase goal* is the *prospecting* target upon which you should focus to achieve your overall sales increase goal.

For example, if you have $1,000,000 in annual sales, you might set a goal of $200,000 total growth in sales, your *overall sales increase goal.* If you expect 10 percent attrition and no growth from your existing customers, your *net annual increase sales goal* will be $300,000—$200,000 of wanted

FIGURE 8.5 Creating the Formula for Targeted Sales Growth

> Attrition + Growth of Existing Business + *Overall Sales Increase Goal* = Net Annual Sales Increase Goal

Note: The goal that salespeople often focus on is the *overall sales increase goal;* they fail to consider the dynamics of their existing customer base. They should estimate the attrition of lost business and the growth of existing customers, to create a net sales goal. The *net sales goal* is the figure upon which additional calculations and intermediate sales objectives can be established.

growth and another $100,000 to replace the business lost to attrition. Or you might have an overall sales increase goal of $200,000 but with the expectation that $150,000 of growth will come from your existing customer base. In this example, your *net annual increase sales goal* would be a mere $50,000, in which case you might consider that you can attain an even loftier goal.[2]

Many different subjective and objective factors have an impact on goal setting, including economic conditions (e.g., housing starts), supplier capacity, market maturation, sales experience, and more. Of the preceding list, the term *market maturation* might arouse your curiosity. Market maturation refers to a supplier's level of experience and penetration in a market. A supplier relatively new to a market might set very modest goals because the supplier will invest a lot of early groundwork in promoting brand awareness. Another supplier who has already made a significant investment in brand promotion might have loftier goals, in spite of modest experience in the market. A supplier with significant brand awareness *and* extensive market penetration might have to be conservative in its growth estimates, citing market saturation as a factor that prevents exponential growth. Numerous obstacles can affect the pursuit of goals. The solution to this ambiguity is to create a simple method that eliminates the uncertain variables and lets you focus on simple targets that ensure successful attainment of your goals.

The formula in Figure 8.6 provides a simple goal-setting calculation that reduces variables and uncertainty. The formula is irrefutable. The closing ratio in Figure 8.6 is based on the percentage of success that is achieved with *new sales opportunities*. It is essential that you distinguish between new sales opportunities and expected sales. You already know that a builder who has purchased from you for four years will probably continue to buy from you in the near future. A builder who has never purchased from you is still a cold prospect. Your expected closing ratio with the former builder is nearly 100 percent, while your expectations with the latter is a matter of uncertainty. It is the latter, new-builder closing ratio that you need to scrutinize and calculate over a period of months and years. And although the historical performance of your closing ratio is no guarantee of the future, it is the best predictor you have available. If you have any doubts about your actual ratio, create a conservative estimate (e.g., 10 percent) to increase your chances for achieving your sales goals. You can express your sales

---

[2] The difference in these two examples illustrates a problem that occurs when an organization attempts to set general goals for individual salespeople. It is not the least bit unusual for an employer or supervisor to issue generic goals across the board to an entire staff of salespeople. An organization that expects 15 percent growth conveniently issues a common goal for all salespeople to achieve 20 percent increases in sales. The organization figures (rightly) that some salespeople will reach the goal and many will not; thus, it hopes that the average results will allow the organization to attain its objectives. This type of goal setting is common among all industries and contributes immensely to salespeople's suffering of want. From our examples and your own experiences, you can easily spot situations in which two similar-looking territories might yield vastly different results.

FIGURE 8.6 100 Percent Guaranteed Method for Achieving Your Sales Goal

<table>
<tr><td colspan="1">

**100 Percent Guaranteed Method for
Achieving Your Sales Goal**

x = Net Sales Increase Goal

y = % Closing Ratio

z = Total Prospecting Activity Needed to Achieve Goal

If $z \times y = x$,

Then $z = x/y$

</td></tr>
</table>

volume of *new business* by multiplying your prospecting sales volume by your closing ratio. That calculation helps you *after* you know how much you have prospected. But how can you establish your target *before* the start of the year?

The process is simpler than you might expect. The *total prospecting activity needed to achieve your overall goal* is the *net sales increase goal divided by your closing ratio.* As an example, if you located $3,000,000 in sales opportunity and sold $450,000, then your closing ratio is 15 percent. ($3,000,000 × .15 = $450,000). Thus, you can predict future performance based upon the same closing ratio. If your closing ratio is 15 percent, and you wish to sell $600,000 more in the following year, you need to complete two simple steps. First, you evaluate your attrition and growth rate with existing customers. For simplicity, assume that these values are both zero. Thus, your sales prospecting goal will be $600,000/.15 = $4,000,000. Although this level of prospecting activity might initially seem insurmountable, there is no need to be concerned. The good news is that you have a finite target within your control. You no longer need to obsess over lost sales and the fear of rejection. Your success is now only a matter of putting forth the effort to make the numbers.

The process may seem complex, but it is actually simple. The variables are minimal—total previous year sales, attrition, and growth from existing customers, overall sales increase goals, and closing ratios. If you conscientiously track these data, you will discover a simple target that makes the accomplishment of your sales goal clear and concise—*the total prospecting activity you need to achieve the goal.*

10. **Eat an elephant one bite at a time.** As salespeople, we often become easily overwhelmed by large goals, especially when those goals require management of millions of sales dollars. The secret to success is to break down larger goals into manageable segments. If you fail to divide your large goals into small tasks, you will certainly be overwhelmed. On the other hand, now that you have determined the larger goals from the previous tactic, the rest of the planning process is simple.

You can divide the annual number by 12 to create a monthly goal, by 50 to create a weekly goal, and by 200 (or the weekly goal divided by 4) to create a daily goal. When you have established daily goals that help you achieve annual objectives, you can easily monitor your progress and activity by focusing on your daily actions.

- Monthly Activity = Total Prospecting Activity/12
- Weekly Activity = Total Prospecting Activity/50 (allowing for a two-week vacation)
- Daily Activity = Weekly Activity/4 (allowing for meetings, emergencies, and administrative tasks)

If you want to increase sales by $600,000, and you are overly focused on the results, you virtually guarantee yourself the suffering of want. If you accurately tracked your previous year's prospecting efforts, you might discover that $1.6 million of sales opportunities is already in the pipeline. You may have discovered that you are going to lose nearly $200,000 from one major customer, but you will replace that loss with nearly $250,000 from another customer; so you can conclude that your attrition rate is pretty close to zero. You therefore are in a simple position to evaluate the small steps you would need to achieve your lofty goal of a one-half-million-dollar increase. You have a 20 percent closing ratio on new business opportunities, and you realize therefore that you need $3,000,000 in sales opportunity to reach your goal (i.e., $600,000/.20=$3,000,000). Because you have $1,600,000 in carryover, the remaining $1,400,000 is an easy goal to achieve. In this case, you wisely raise your goal, recognizing that some opportunities often take up to six months to develop. You eventually settle on a total annual goal of $2,400,000: $200,000 per month, $48,000 per week, $12,000 per day. What a wonderful feeling you will have every day as you discover new sales opportunities. Your goals are broken down into manageable "bites" that give you an excitement every morning for which many salespeople would be envious. A formerly insurmountable goal now seems almost too easy to achieve.

Use the tactics from this chapter to establish realistic sales goals, and break those goals down into manageable steps. You will then achieve a new level of confidence and joy for the profession of selling. Your ability to achieve goals no longer will be predicated on the whims of customers, employers, or coworkers. The beauty of this methodology is that it lets you achieve your sales goal by simply focusing on one single day, each day. If you want healthy teeth, you have to brush and floss every day. An intense session of brushing the night before a dental appointment will not fool your hygienist. Similarly, if you want to achieve annual sales goals, you must determine what activity is required each day to take you to your destination. Confucius said a thousand-mile journey begins with a single step. Your pursuit of sales goals is similar: Each single step is a simple task that takes you toward a worthy destination.

CHAPTER NINE

ELIMINATING
SUFFERING AND TAKING CONTROL

As salespeople, we spend more than half of our waking hours at work. We are defined by jobs that are far too often a source of suffering, fear, and anger. The first question we are often asked at a cocktail party is not "What hobbies or interests do you have?" but rather "What do you do?" Eventually, we realize there is no realistic way to completely detach our work life from our "real" life. Many of us live for the weekends, waiting for the moment when we can say, "Thank God, it's Friday!" This signifies the end to a week of drudgery sandwiched in between life's enjoyment. Wednesday is "hump day," the day at which we are halfway through the agony of a workweek. This sad perspective creates problems that extend well beyond the workplace. We cannot separate the suffering and frustration we experience in the workplace from our real life. We cannot achieve happiness in our lives until we eliminate suffering in the workplace.

I wrote this book to help you eliminate suffering in your career, although it leaves a few questions still unanswered. Can you completely eliminate suffering? What if you can only reduce it? Is suffering real or perceived? How can you deal with the obstacles of angry customers, bad company policy, irritable coworkers, unfair bosses, and other unpleasantness? The answers to these questions are that, more often than not, your own fears and insecurities cause suffering. You ultimately choose the degree of your own suffering. You can reduce suffering by choosing to change your behaviors and decisions. You can often eliminate suffering by simply choosing to change your perspective. This book provides you with sales ideas that will relieve career suffering and frustration. More importantly, it provides the foundation for you to create more of your own ideas, for its real purpose is to help you foster a new way to think about your career and life.

The first part of the book shares several vital points with you. It is designed to heighten your awareness of immense industry challenges—the construction industry and human interactions are complex. Because there is so much diversity, you must prepare for the variety of situations and audiences that you will encounter. You must prepare yourself for the many tasks in your dual roles of promotional sales and product sales. Preparation, as the word implies, must take place before you step onto the field of battle. It is too late to plan during the heat of battle. Recognition of the obstacles enables you to develop a vision that fosters success and happiness.

The second part of the book identifies four distinct audiences—builders, architects, dealers, and salespeople—and offers detailed strategies and tactics to use with each. By now, you surely realize that the strategies and tactics are much larger in scope. You can, for instance, employ the strategy of slowing down not only with builders but also in a vast array of other circumstances. You can employ the strategy of becoming a sales manager by mentoring any coworker, customer, associate, or supervisor. I make no claim that these strategies represent all of the strategies available. I make no boast that the tactics provide you with every skill you will ever need. However, I can promise one thing: If you strive to consciously employ the strategies and tactics in this book, you will grow. If you will honestly appraise your own performance and strive to improve whenever possible, you will create alignment between your values and behaviors, your strategies and tactics. Eventually you will develop your own new strategies and tactics, which will give you more growth and security than you ever thought possible . . . and, of course, more happiness in your career.

The final part of the book offers you help in minimizing the fear that inevitably creeps in. You can discover ways to decrease your suffering at work and therefore increase your overall happiness in life. However, in spite of your desire to eliminate bad emotions, you will probably still have bad days that result from insecurities and worries. It's tempting during those bad days to give up, to conclude that you will continually experience the negative emotions you feel at a particular moment. When those feelings occur, be gentle and remind yourself that, even after a bout of fear or anger, you can let the bad thoughts dissolve and start all over again. Your transition from fear to courage is not an event, but rather a process. You may never completely eliminate bad emotions. But you can renew your battle every day, and strive for happiness and joy, and love the journey along the way.

How to Overcome Fear

To overcome your fears, develop your skills with the following tactics:

1. Do what your fear most. Long ago, fear was an adaptive behavior that aided the survival of primitive humans, a fight-or-flight response triggered by the medulla oblongata to immediate threats. Fear was (and remains) a re-action to actual threats, but it has evolved to include responses to imagined threats, as well. Fear grips emotions and stifles activity. Humans fear the unknown and the consequences of experimental activities.

10 TACTICS THAT HELP YOU OVERCOME FEAR

1. Do what your fear most.
2. Practice. Practice. Practice.
3. Review your performance continuously.
4. Invent new tactics.
5. Invent new strategies.
6. Give your knowledge freely.
7. Measure your overall performance.
8. Change your view of the past.
9. Change your outlook for the future.
10. Live in the moment.

The key to overcome many forms of fear is to engage in new activities and risk the outcome you fear most. Do the very thing that you fear, and one of two things will happen: You will discover that the consequences you fear never come to pass, or they do. More often than not, the consequences that you fear will never materialize. If they do, you can deal with them while you learn from the experience.

If you fear the action of holding firm on your price, then hold your price, and learn that you do not always lose the sale (the consequence you feared). If you fear the silence of accepting a customer's tirade, then remain silent, and discover that your customer actually loses momentum and, in the process, gains respect for you (a better consequence than you had expected). If you hate your job and want to quit, resolve to make it better by not quitting, particularly if you have a history of job-hopping.

Ask yourself what consequences you fear from your actions, and then take action. Your heart will initially rebel, and your mind will need to over-ride instinct. Once your mind has taken control, you will discover that fear subsides and courage replaces it. Your heart ultimately feels better for the decision your mind made. Mark Twain once said, "Courage is not the absence of fear, but is the mastery of it." Do what you fear most to overcome your fear.

2. Practice. Practice. Practice. You have probably heard the joke many times: The tourist hops in the cab and asks the driver, "Do you know how to get to Carnegie Hall?" The cabbie looks over his shoulder and advises the passenger, "Practice. Practice. Practice."

Great musicians and athletes have a knack for emerging as clutch performers because of their ability to remain calm in pressure situations. Their calm and confidence during peak-performance moments is created by the persistent practice of their skill over the course of many years, often since childhood. They recognize the need to practice a single task hundreds, if not thousands, of times before they develop the necessary skills for success in their field. They know that proper technique will eventually create the desired results and the ability to perform under pressure.

Great salespeople emerge in the same way as great artists and athletes. They discover ways to practice the job of selling. Unfortunately, however, there is no "practice time" in business like there is in art and sport. Thus, the star performers in business discover ways to practice *on the job*. Most salespeople underestimate the need for practice, instead focusing on the results of their effort. They evaluate their performance solely by focusing on the *outcome* and rarely focusing on the *task*, a certain recipe for fear. If you focus solely on the results, you will discover that fear becomes the persistent bane of your existence. Focusing solely on results creates tension and bad sales technique. You must use "game time" for the purpose of both playing (measuring your results) and practicing (evaluating your skills) at the same time.

Change your work philosophy and recognize that you are always working and practicing simultaneously. If you let yourself think about work as practice time, you will discover that your game-time results eventually improve. Use the next tactic to improve your practice sessions.

3. **Review your performance continuously.** A common, subconscious fear for salespeople is that their success is accidental. Even when they achieve the desired results, they have a nagging thought that luck, not their own intention, may have been the catalyst for success. In other words, even when things go well, they feel unsure of their ability to achieve the same results again. If you have similar experiences, careful self-observation of your performance will create confidence in your ability to repeat a task. At the conclusion of every meeting, ask yourself two questions:

- What went well?
- What could I have done better?

The answer to the first question will tell you what behaviors to repeat in the future. If you had a particularly successful meeting, pinpoint the reasons for the success. Your future performance will be enhanced and your future meetings will become more purposeful. The answer to the second question provides you with ideas that will help you avoid the repetition of mistakes. The common wisdom of *focusing only on the positive* is a wonderful thought, but unfortunately this approach does nothing to correct poor performance. Sometimes one needs to observe the negative to learn from it. If you are fully committed to personal growth, you will ask yourself *both* of these questions continually. The practice of asking (and objectively answering) these two questions provides a foundation for growth that reduces fear.

4. **Invent new tactics.** This book offers 100 tactics to help you become more effective in your career. But these tactics are far from all encompassing. In fact, there is an abundance of opportunity to invent new tactics and

behaviors every day. Most salespeople who employ the skills of strategic sell-ing begin to develop their own tactics to support various strategies. Try inventing new tactics for some of the strategies in this book. For example, if you want to get more salespeople involved (Strategy #7), then invite sales-people of noncompeting companies to a regular breakfast meeting for the purpose of exchanging valuable sales leads. If you want to slow down the process (Strategy #1), invite a builder or an architect to your showroom for a tour.

I am disappointed when I hear (frequently) the statement from people, "There are no new ideas in sales training . . . It's all the same stuff repack-aged in different ways." This perspective is ridiculous. New ideas are being invented every day for offering presentations, asking questions, improving prospecting, enhancing technology, delivering feedback, expressing empa-thy, developing assertiveness, overcoming writer's block, listening, build-ing rapport, handling objections, cultivating negotiation techniques, and more . . . and more! Somewhere in the middle of the nineteenth century, the head of the US Patent office retired because "everything had been invented." In the 1980s, a popular magazine noted that the computer indus-try was in trouble and had nowhere to grow. The next time you think there are no new ideas, remind yourself that innovation is what distinguishes man from beasts. Create your own innovations to stay ahead of the competition.

5. **Invent new strategies.** While you are inventing new tactics, try a few new strategies as well. Here is a good strategy: *React to trends, not events.* Salespeople are notorious for reacting to a single statement from a disgrun-tled customer, or a negative event during a sales meeting. Don't let your bad day create an overreaction. React to trends and situations. Some tactics that support this strategy include the following:

- When you receive a complaint, try counting the times it recurs to determine whether it represents a legitimate trend.
- When you receive a special product request, take the request under advisement before you recommend a major investment in product engineering.
- Count the number of special requests, to spot the trends.

See how many other tactics you can create for this strategy.

Here is another sound strategy: *Create a specific purpose for every meeting.* Tactics include the following:

- Get a follow-up appointment.
- Deliver a quote in person.
- Share a new piece of literature.
- Discover more about your customer's business.
- Discuss market trends.
- Share information on a new regulatory issue.

You can invent numerous tactics to support this strategy. Invent some more. A meeting without a specific business purpose is nothing more than a social conversation and a poor investment in everyone's time. The more you practice inventing new strategies and corresponding tactics, the more prepared you will be for the heat of battle.

6. **Give your knowledge freely.** If you want to learn, teach. Many people hoard knowledge to retain control over others. Yet there is no better way to become proficient at a skill than teaching it. There is also no better way to become a leader than to share your knowledge. A famous example of this, once again, was Ben Franklin. Ben was an inventor, an avid investigator of science, a successful businessman, an athlete (in his younger years, he was an avid swimmer), and a charming man who became an important diplomat for the United States during the American Revolution. Ben's contributions to science and social consciousness are well documented. You might be surprised to learn that Ben rarely profited from his contributions. In fact, he was of the opinion that there should be no monopoly on scientific innovation and intellectual property. The unselfish generosity with which he offered his intellectual contributions made him one of the most revered human beings in the history of the United States. Of course, one should also strive to avoid sharing knowledge solely for the purpose of boastfulness. Ben also warned us, "He is a fool who cannot conceal his wisdom." The real power of knowledge is the ability to share ideas with others to lead them in their personal journeys of growth.

7. **Measure your overall performance.** The previous chapter shared numerous ideas on how to measure your performance, both your activity and the results of that activity. But to *think* about measuring performance is not enough; you have to do it. Measuring performance is not a *sometimes* thing; it is an *always* thing. If you want to create a perfect performance, then you must sweat every little detail. Imagine the struggle that the pointillist painter Georges Seurat endured as he made massive canvasses of beautiful impressionist art by painting one individual dot at a time. That is the struggle of the expert salesperson. You will never be able to measure your overall performance until you have successfully quantified the small details. At the end of every meeting, update your database notes. If you obtain a new lead, put it on your lead-tracking list. At the end of every week, count the number of appointments you made. At the conclusion of the month, evaluate your sales, leads, appointment activity, and any other data that can help you improve. Sweat the details, measure your performance, and then allow the artist in you to step back and evaluate the canvas of your work.

8. **Change your view of the past.** Psychological studies have shown that past *experiences* are not what mold our impressions. Rather, it is our *interpretation* of past experiences. One man who went bankrupt stated that he had learned a valuable lesson from the experience. He felt that his dealings in business that led up to his bankruptcy taught him how to become successful, and he knew he would rise again. Another man wallowed in sadness after his bankruptcy and was never again satisfied with his monetary wealth. One salesman recalls a bad day he once had because he lost an

important sale, while another declares how much he learned from a similar experience; the former counts his lost income, while the latter calculates his future earnings potential. Your *interpretation* of your past, not the events themselves, determines your happiness and satisfaction with your past.

9. **Change your outlook for the future.** The future is dark and unknown, exciting and terrifying, all at the same time. One thing is certain: There is an abundance of opportunity in the world. You are alive at a time when travel around the globe in one day is possible. You live in a time when technology provides conveniences never before experienced during the history of mankind. You live in a time of enlightenment that affords you opportunities to discover deep understanding of spirituality, meditation, exercise, literature, business, nature, science, and nearly anything else you would like to know. You live in a time during which many people take the basic necessities of food, shelter, and clothing for granted while they harbor fear of the future. Your sense of optimism will be enhanced if you commit to an ongoing regimen of personal growth and awareness. Money, title, and material wealth will not improve your outlook on the future. Your ability to help yourself and others grow is the greatest gift any person can possess. Commit yourself to a future of personal growth and discovery, and you will develop unshakable optimism.

10. **Live in the moment.** There is no sense dwelling in the past, because it is over. We can learn from the past, and then release it, and nothing more. There is little sense to fear the future or to strive to make outlandish predictions about it. The future, for the most part, is out of our control. *Opportunity is when preparation meets luck.* We can only prepare ourselves for the future by striving for personal growth in the very moment we are living. Now. This moment. There is only this moment. We must make each sales meeting the best meeting. When we are with a customer, there is only that customer. We live in a world of distractions, where people talk on their cell phones while regretting their behavior in a past sales meeting at the same time as they worry about a pending sale on their way to pick up their children from soccer practice. The worries of the past and future distract our attention from the living moment, the only moment over which we can exert control.

If you've gained nothing else from this book, hopefully you have discovered that fear is reduced when you create purpose for your actions. Focus on one single action at a time. If you feel that you've made a mistake, learn from it. If you know you are experiencing a winning moment, take time to wallow in your success, to both enjoy the moment and learn to repeat it later. You can do only one action at any given time. Do that action to the best of your ability, and enjoy the moment. Lord Byron said, "Live each day as though it will be your last. One day you're certain to be right."

Live as though you will die tomorrow.

Learn as though you will live forever.

CUSTOMER TRACKING

Most salespeople know the importance of tracking customer purchases. The spreadsheet in this appendix allows salespeople to track the purchases of their customers. It is recommended that you plan to estimate future purchases from individual customers, discussing those goals with customers whenever appropriate. Tracking customer purchases will enable you to make predictions about future attrition rates and important trends in your market. Your use of this spreadsheet will help you become a better manager of your activity and results. You will instinctively create adjustments to the spreadsheet that make the tool more effective for you.

The following guidelines should help you utilize the spreadsheet as it appears. You can adjust the data to suit your own needs.

Customer Rating—This information should give you a simple code (e.g., A, B, C) by which to evaluate account potential. Your customers' actual purchases will help you adjust your ratings and time-management methods.

Account Name—The name of the account.

Previous Year Sales—The level of sales from the year prior to the one you will be tracking. This information lets you sort your customers by volume. It will also provide guidelines by which you can establish accurate projections for future purchases.

Current Year Projections—The level of sales you expect, your sales goal, for individual customers. If you persistently overestimate sales projections, you will gain a visual perspective from the spreadsheet. You may also discover that your projections are overly pessimistic. Most salespeople expect that they will easily make accurate projections, but they often discover that the task is more challenging than they expected. Accurate tracking of this data will improve over time.

(+ or −)—A numeric value that the spreadsheet can calculate for you or that you can enter manually. You may choose to use a percentage or an actual dollar figure. The purpose of tracking this value is to help you establish realistic goals and visualize trends.

Reason for Expected Change—This information becomes more than a good communication tool between you and your supervisor; it is an important method for rationalizing your projections. Many salespeople overestimate sales projections to justify lofty sales goals. This column helps you determine whether you are properly justifying your sales goals.

Customer Tracking—You should determine whether you want to measure your performance on a monthly or quarterly basis. Quarterly tracking lets you observe trends more accurately, while monthly tracking permits rapid adjustments to you activity. The importance of tracking your individual customer purchases cannot be overestimated. You should regularly compare actual purchases to projections to monitor your progress during the year.

CUSTOMER TRACKING FORM

Account Rating	Account Name	Previous Year Sales	Current Year Projections	Projected Increase (or Decrease)	Reason for expected change	TOTAL		1st Quarter		2nd Quarter		3rd Quarter		4th Quarter	
						Projected	Actual	Projected	Actual	Projected	Actual	Projected	Actual	Projected	Actual
Totals															

GLOSSARY

account lead—The offer of an ongoing relationship.

analytical buyer—As the name implies, is focused on technical issues related to data and scientific analysis of products and services.

appointment—Simply what one would consider a traditional meeting that has been scheduled for a specific date and time and, hopefully, with a planned purpose.

attrition—The erosion of your customer base that occurs as a result of lost customers or decreasing purchases from retained accounts.

big-box retailer—A national or regional dealer of building materials that caters to the do-it-yourself consumer, but may also have contractor sales capabilities (e.g. Home Depot, Lowes, etc.)

box lunch—A scheduled presentation during which the staff of an architectural firm listens to a product presentation while eating lunch that is provided by the presenters.

Certified Kitchen Designer (CKD)—A specialist in the cabinet industry who helps dealerships adapt to special product knowledge and sales challenges.

cold call—A meeting or phone call to a prospect who has no expectation of the visit.

combative negotiators—Adopt the strategy that their suppliers should be held responsible for as much as possible. Their strategy is simply to avoid commitments to suppliers and sell whatever the customer asks for. In other words, the combative dealer prefers to develop situations in which they have access to as many product brands as possible.

compromising negotiators—Adopt the strategy to cultivate relationships with manufacturers that provide good products, dependable service, and financial stability. They recognize that they owe some degree of loyalty to suppliers. While compromising dealers may not aggressively promote product brands, they are at least participants in the programs offered by suppliers.

construction documents—In the construction document stage, the final drawings, specifications, and other related documents are prepared for the next stage, the bid.

cooperative negotiators—Employ the strategy by which they aggressively strive to partner with suppliers to maximize market shares. They seek relationships in which suppliers want to partner to outsell local competitors.

customer bid closing ratio—The percentage of bids sold to existing customers.

design development—During the design development phase, specific details of the project are determined and product choices are discussed.

design phase—The overall total design phase of a project, inclusive of schematic design, design development, and construction documentation.

direct sales—Sales to builders or contractors without the use of a middle man.

farming—Sales management of existing customer accounts. The primary focus of this sales style is to stabilize relationships with existing customers and achieve sales growth.

fast buyer—Is the most aggressive type of customer, seeking immediate results while the power buyer, also seeking results, is focused on the bigger picture of long-term benefit.

feature-benefit (FAB)—The common method of product presentation in which a salesperson lists a feature and then states a benefit of that feature. The misuse of this popular approach has created many presentations in which salespeople are presenting features that may not necessarily be important to the listener.

friendly buyer—Is interested in long-term relationships; and is more interested in personal rapport.

hunting—The proactive pursuit of new customers (i.e. pure prospecting).

inside salespeople—Salespeople for a dealer that works at a counter and rarely makes calls to customers and prospects outside of the dealer office.

lead—Any sales opportunity that can be quantified.

Lead-Valuation Method—Designed solely to measure the value of sales opportunities and monitor their progress.

macroeconomics—The study of the national and international economies.

Macrosales theory—Focuses on managing the bigger picture. Macrosales strategies focus on the activities that allow you to plan entire weeks, months, and years of activity.

market maturation—Refers to a supplier's level of experience and penetration in a market.

microeconomics—The study of individual business operations.

Microsales theory—Focuses on the one-on-one relationship between the supplier and the customer. Microsales strategies are therefore focused on the plans and actions that increase your sales success with individual customers and prospects.

net sales increase goal—Includes consideration for both attrition and growth from your existing customer base.

one-step distribution (distributor)—A wholesale dealer of building materials that engages in direct sales to builders and contractors.

outside salespeople—Salespeople for a dealer that works primarily outside of the office, meeting prospects and customers at their business locations.

overall sales increase goal—The sales volume over your previous end-of-year totals.

personal growth—The proactive pursuit of knowledge and personal selling skills.

product quality—Is naturally an important factor in purchasing decisions. What constitutes product quality is less clear. In some cases, brand recognition is enough to establish product quality. Some builders prefer to install popular products into their homes even in lieu of better products that are offered at a lower price.

power buyer—Is interested in long-term relationships, and is more likely to focus on business issues.

profit model—Is the value of the transactions and business relationship between the supplier and customer.

project lead—The offer of an immediate sale for your customer. A project lead can evolve into a more general account lead.

project sales—This sales role defines salespeople in the process of selling directly to builders or architects.

promotional sales—This sales role defines salespeople engaged in the task of selling to customers who resell products.

prospect bid closing ratio—The percentage of bids sold to prospects, measured by total volume.

prospect closing ratio—The percentage of new customers gained from a list of prospects.

quantification—The calculation and measurement of value, activity, and performance. The purpose of quantification is to enable one to measure otherwise indefinable activities and values (Example: One salesperson states that they were very busy the previous week while another salesperson states that they had 26 meetings with prospects and customers. The former salesperson is making a value judgment while the latter is quantifying performance.)

sales blitz—A sales event in which a group of salespeople target a geographic area with intensive prospecting efforts.

schematic design—During schematic design, the owner and the architect determine what the style and function of a project will include. They determine budget constraints and physical limitations of the project.

specification—A recommended selection of a product, not the sale itself.

strategy—A game plan that guides you to the accomplishment of an objective.

tactic—An action that can support and fulfill the strategy.

transaction—The sale.

transfer of training—The successful implementation of a training lesson.

two-step distribution—Wholesale distribution of building materials where a merchant sells to a wholesale dealer, which will in turn re-sell materials to a contractor or builder, thus creating "two steps" between the manufacturer and the builder (i.e. Manufacturer→Distributor→ Dealer→Builder).

warm call—A meeting with a customer who at least has the expectation of a meeting, although no time for the meeting has been specifically scheduled.

value-added—A common term used by salespeople to imply the offer of a profit model. The difference between selling a "profit model" and "value added" is that the former includes actual calculation of value while the latter is an unverified claim that the salesperson expects the customer to accept.